PERFORMANCE SKILLS FOR AMATEUR DRAMA

ANN MOORE

Performance Skills for Amateur Drama

First published in England 2015
by Eyelevel Books, Worcester
www.eyelevelbooks.co.uk

©2016

Copyright © Ann Moore 2014
Foreword © Bill Maynard 2007
Illustrations © Diane Cope 2007

The right of contributors to be identified as the authors of this work has been asserted by them in accordance with the Copyright, Designs and Patents Act 1998.
All rights reserved. No part of this publication may be reproduced, stored or introduced into a retrieval system or transmitted in any form or by any means without the prior written permission of the publisher.

Typeset and Designed by Eyelevel Books.

PREFACE

Performance Skills for Amateur Drama is a practical guide for drama group leaders who want to improve stage skills and get the most out of group meetings. Following on from the companion volumes **How to Set up and Amateur Drama Group** and **How to Stage a Play**, this book contains dozens of fun exercises to aid group cohesion, confidence and relaxation. Later exercises work on specific skills including breath control, vocal expression, body language and improvisation.

These tips and techniques are drawn from over fifty years' experience both in amateur and professional theatre and will form an invaluable foundation for any group wanting to maximise the pleasure and satisfaction to be enjoyed from public performance – both for the group themselves, and their audience!

These three books can also be found in the single volume, '**Beginners Please**' (print edition ISBN 9781902528236, or as an ebook exclusively on Amazon).

CONTENTS

	Foreword by Bill Maynard	7
	Author's Note	8
1	**Practical Skills**	**9**
	Acquiring Skills – an introduction	9
	Tips for the leader	10
	Choosing 'teams'	10
2	**Warm-ups**	**12**
	…also known as ice-breakers	12
	Circle games	13
	Space Activities	14
	Space and imagination activities	15
	Individual	15
	Partner/Group Space activities	18
	Partners	18
	In groups	20
3	**Concentrate!**	**22**
	The Need for Concentration	22
	Partners	22
	In Groups	24
4	**Relax…**	**27**
	the need for relaxation	27
	Standing exercises	28
	The whole body	29
	Head and neck and shoulders	30
	Posture	30
5	**Performance Skills 1**	**32**
	Vocal performance skills	32
	Breath control	32
	Partners	34
	In groups	34
	Articulation	35
	Vocal expression	38
	Projection	41

6	**Performance Skills 2**	**43**
	Physical performance skills	43
	Body language	43
	Eye contact	44
	Facial expression	45
	Creating character physically	45
	Memory and Imagination	49
7	**Creative Drama**	**51**
	Improvisation and Mime	51
	Improvisation	51
	Mime	53
	Individual mime	54
	Collective Mime	55
	Partner and group mimes	57
8	**Improvised Drama**	**60**
	Improvised drama	60
	Individual Activities	60
	Partners	61
	With a partner – Vocal	62
	Group work	66
	'Open' ideas	66
	Further 'open' ideas	67
	Locations	68
	Play-making	68
	A Theme	70
	Using known material as a starting point	70
	Texts for large groups	72
	Costume/properties which suggest a character	73
	Conclusion	75
	Appendix: useful websites	**77**
	Legal and Statutory Bodies	77
	Sources of General Help and Inspiration	77
	Sources of Plays and Other Material	78

ACKNOWLEDGMENTS

I should like to express my thanks to the following: Jon at Eyelevel Books for suggesting that I write the book in the first place and for his subsequent encouragement and patience; to Diane Cope for her delightful drawings; to John Hackett for his suggestions and for proof-reading; to Shiela Hodges and Jake Chambers for checking some of the information. For their valued support in this project I must also thank the veteran professional actor Bill Maynard and the Chairman of the Independent Theatre Council, Gavin Stride, who are both great advocates of amateur participation in the arts. I must also mention the actors and directors, both amateur and professional with whom, over the years, I have enjoyed the happiest of times and from whom I learned so much. Finally my thanks must go to my family who allowed me time and space, not only to pursue my interests in drama, but also to produce this book.

ABOUT THE AUTHOR

Ann Moore has been involved with drama for more than fifty years, experiencing most aspects of the art, from acting to stage management, props to directing.

Working with both amateurs and professionals, she has acted in more than fifty plays, from Alan Ayckbourn and Agatha Christie to Shakespeare and Arnold Wesker.

She has directed regularly for the last thirty years – and still does – and has taught drama to Secondary School pupils and adults.

She is an active member of two Performing Arts groups, one of which is based in a professional theatre, and she recently established a thriving drama society in her local community.

FOREWORD BY BILL MAYNARD

Having spent a lifetime as a professional in most aspects of the entertainment business, I read this guide to amateur drama by Ann Moore with great interest.

This straightforward, all-embracing manual is perfect for anyone who is interested in the stage as a hobby but has little experience. Yet there are ideas here which would interest the more experienced members of an amateur drama group too – and the tips are not just for actors. The spotlight of information is turned on all aspects of amateur drama, from starting up a group in the first place to staging a production and covering everything from improvising acting skills to the work of the director and stage management and to those involved with their audience front-of-house.

Whatever your interest in amateur drama you'll find ideas in this manual which will help you to enjoy not only the fun and friendship, but also the *success*, as you share your love of the stage to bring live theatre into your community.

Bill Maynard

AUTHOR'S NOTE

Every actor and every director has his own way of working and in writing this book I pass on ideas which have worked for me and for many others, both amateur and professional with whom I have been associated in drama. Take from them what you will.

In an attempt to avoid over-long and cumbersome descriptions, I have compromised in my use of pronouns. I have often referred, for example, to the Director as 'he'; to the Stage Manager as 'she'; and so on. This should not be taken as bias and readers should never infer that these, or any other, roles are better suited to one or the other. All jobs, from committee chair and director right through to coffee-server and programme seller are, and should be, considered as equally suitable for *anyone* with the skill and willingness to undertake them.

Amateur Drama is one of the most democratic and inclusive art-forms and it is a place to leave politics and prejudice at the door. Disability, colour, educational background or sex are no barrier to participation within any of the huge range of jobs necessary to bring drama to the stage. For both participants and audience it should be the fun and life-enhancing experience which I have always found it to be. The stage is a world of dreams where anything is possible, whoever you are.

So, Beginners, Please, take your place, have fun and let the dream begin…

1 PRACTICAL SKILLS

what this chapter covers...

This chapter forms an introduction to a series of chapters dealing with the practical side of drama group meetings. The games and exercises which follow form the backbone of such meetings, and are designed to be both fun and invaluable for developing the skills needed for performance.

ACQUIRING SKILLS – AN INTRODUCTION

In this section we look at activities which can be used by members of all ages in any amateur drama group, activities which are not only fun to do, but which will also help those involved to grow in confidence as well as in drama skills. As they share these activities, members will get to know each other better and learn to trust each other, and at the same time build a confidence, which will enable them to try something new and succeed in it. In particular, these exercises and improvisations should help an amateur actor learn techniques which will help improve his performance on stage. A good actor needs to know how to use concentration, imagination and observation if he is to succeed. He must be able to use both physical and vocal expression to good effect, to enjoy working as a member of a team, sharing ideas, summoning the confidence and energy to bring a written character to life. The activities in this section will foster these skills, but above all, all members of a social drama group should find that if they take part, even if just for enjoyment, they will still benefit in some way.

The following chapters should also help a drama leader to fashion an entertaining evening for members of his group. The ideas can be mixed and matched so as to provide fun, as well as perhaps targeting a particular area of expertise or skill needed in a current or forthcoming production, although only the organiser may be aware of this objective. It is expected that members will be asked to 'show' what they've done, especially in partner or group work (and especially if the leader has seen that it's good), but no member should be forced to do so if he feels his work isn't ready for 'performance'. Some activities lend themselves to this better than others, and there's not always sufficient time for a great deal of 'showing', but a group pleased with its efforts will want to share their work with fellow members. This should be encouraged, for it's an opportunity to illustrate not only individual growth, but also the ability to work in partnership with others, and it provides an opportunity for positive discussion and mutual enjoyment.

Throughout, the instructions are given as if to the individual so that they may be taken by one person, or used by a leader.

TIPS FOR THE LEADER

Do make sure, especially with a new group, that all the activities you choose to do are suitable for the membership. However enthusiastic you are, you must expect a certain amount of reticence from some members, especially if at first they don't see the point of what they're being asked to do, or feel that they're being asked to do something which might show them in an unfavourable light. It's unlikely, for instance, that men in a prison group would co-operate if you began by introducing 'Little Peter Rabbit' as a warm-up or concentration exercise! Show understanding, don't coerce, and gradually, as trust and confidence build, everyone will want to join in and you can become more ambitious.

Plan ahead and make sure that you have beside you enough material or ideas to fill the time. Know what you hope to do in any one session. It's better to have too much material than not enough, for an activity may not work as you'd thought it would and so may you may need an alternative exercise. Be aware of how much time you intend to give to each activity but be prepared to be flexible. Timing does get easier with practice, especially as the group consolidates.

Never give instructions until members are quiet and ready to listen. They should also be reminded to listen for your voice as they work, so that they don't miss further instructions. After all, listening is one of the most important aspects of stage work.

CHOOSING 'TEAMS'

As leader you may often find when you call for individual members to form couples or small groups that, like children playing team games, the same people will come together each time, but this negates the idea of learning to work with someone else, whoever he may be. Although it's to be expected that friend will partner friend at first, there are several ways of making sure that this doesn't happen on a regular basis to the exclusion of someone who may be reticent or new to the group. If you do use any of the following suggestions, don't explain why you're asking members to do as you ask. Make it more of a *'how quickly can you…'* game so that in the scramble to get into position, any barriers will be swept away by the desire to succeed. Once you've arranged the group as you wish, you can then proceed with whatever activity you had in mind.

For a **partnered activity** individuals could be asked to line up in order of height or birth month or in alphabetical order of the initial of their first name or surname, for example. Once in line, you can then move them into two lines so that each is facing someone who will be his partner – or 'cut' the lines into the group numbers you want.

As members move round the room at the end of an individual exercise, you could demand that they quickly form a **group** (of whatever number is required) by joining with those immediately nearest to them, or with those who are wearing the same colour, live in the same street, have the same eye or hair colour or shoe size, have the same birth month, had toast for breakfast – whatever you're able to choose through your knowledge of the membership. Very soon, everyone will become used to working with everyone else, new friendships will grow and all members will feel secure and a true member of a happy social group – which, after all, was one of the aims of the steering committee in the first place.

The order and choice of work from any section is obviously down to personal preference.

2 WARM-UPS

what this chapter covers...

In this chapter we explore some games which will prove valuable in both the early days of your drama group (to get members familiar with each other) and later on in preparing participants for more 'in depth' work.

...ALSO KNOWN AS ICE-BREAKERS

These activities are very useful as a way of breaking the ice for members of a newly formed group, as well as bringing members together at the start of a meeting. They foster friendship and a willingness to join in and be part of the group in whatever it may be doing next. This is especially true if the leader introduces the activity in a spirit of fun and, at first, joins in himself. In many cases these activities do also literally 'warm up' participants – especially on a winter evening – loosening up their muscles and relaxing them. So, warm-ups are valuable in that they not only relax the members physically, but they help concentration and create a friendly cohesion within the group, and this cohesion will carry through to other activities and even into stage performance.

Below is a selection of ideas which have proved to be successful, but of course you'll only use those which you consider most suitable for your group and the space they are in. These activities will, hopefully, prove a springboard for other ideas you may have.

Physical warm ups should generally be used one at a time, or two at the most, and never extended to the onset of boredom – or exhaustion! Another separate exercise, physical or vocal (a concentration or relaxation game perhaps) could follow before embarking on the main activity for the evening.

At all times you should be in control and aware of whether the exercises are being enjoyed or not.

CIRCLE GAMES

You could try 'The Hokey Kokey' dance, of course, or where music is available, The Twist, or a traditional circle dance as a 'warm-up' exercise, but the following are great ice-breakers. These too require music (piano or recorded) in the form of either a march or a jaunty tune. If no music is available everyone could sing or hum a song which they all know, as they walk or march, while you call out the changes.

CIRCLE CHAT

Members are asked to form two lines of equal numbers, so that each member is standing behind or in front of another.

Each line breaks to form its own circle **A** and **B**, one inside the other, members **A** facing someone in **B**.

Music begins: those in **A** walk round to their left, **B** to their right.

After a short interval the music stops and each member turns to the member opposite him in the other circle to exchange a remark, whatever comes into their heads – it could be anything from 'My names is …' to 'What on earth are we doing this for?'

The exercise is repeated quickly several times, with circles occasionally being asked to change direction as well. Variations can be used when, for example, instead of a random remark, members are asked to name their favourite food or television programme, what they had for breakfast or where they were born – anything as long as it's not too personal or invasive.

CIRCLE CHANGE

Circles as before, but when the music stops, and on the command 'change', members in **A** and **B** change places quickly, without speaking, so that they're in the other circle.

1. At first they continue to move in the direction of those in their new circle (ie, the opposite direction to that which they were originally moving in). Repeat two or three times, each time changing from inner to outer circle. The more frequent the 'change' call, the more fun it creates.

2. Repeat the above but command that they change circles **and** that each circle changes direction. NB. Don't allow members too long to change places, and again make the changes frequent. This will then involve another acting skill, *concentration*!

Circle Chain

While standing in two-circle formation as above, everyone from circle **A** moves to stand to the right of his opposite number in **B**.

Then each **A** and **B** face each other and touch right hands. As the music starts, all move round in the direction they face in a circle chain, first touching right hands with the person they meet and then left alternately, always moving forward, until everyone can move fluently. Stop.

Repeat the chain. This time, without stopping the flow or the music the leader commands, several times, that everyone turns to walk in the opposite direction. Few manage this without a muddle and laughter!

Circle Dance

The group surrounds one in the middle who repeats a single repetitive step – in time to the music if it is being used – a dance step which everyone else must copy. At your signal, the centre member changes places with whosoever he chooses, who must then in turn continue the 'dance' by inventing another repetitive movement for all to copy.

The circle could be broken into line by your calling out a member's name. He must then lead the group into the 'follow my leader' game, using different movements until you call for him to lead them to a halt, when the 'leader' is changed, or they return to their seats.

SPACE ACTIVITIES

These are activities introduced after each member has found a space in the room to stand in. When he is on stage, an actor should be aware of the space he occupies in relation to the others he is working with, so that he neither masks another, nor has to make a move to avoid him because he has misjudged a spatial area. These exercises, as they progress, help spatial awareness. The first two games are most suitable for young members, for they are very energetic, but even then, care should be taken if they're working on a slippery floor.

Stick in the Mud

This is a chasing game, with one member chosen as 'tag'. On the word *go* the 'tag' member tries to touch as many of the others as he can, so sticking them to the spot. They must stand still until another member frees them by tapping them on the shoulder. After a few minutes, stop and repeat with a different member tagging. The winner after two or three bouts is the 'tagger' who had the most members frozen to the spot when the game finally ends.

TAILS

Each member needs a ribbon, which can be tucked at the waist like a tail. Having found a space and on the command Go, they chase each other round the room, collecting as many 'tails' as they can until they hear 'stop'. Then the winner is the one who holds the most tails.

Standing Warm-ups, such as physical training exercise (of the 'arms stretch, knees bend' type) can be done if you have a particularly young and energetic group, but the most successful 'ice-breakers' are activities which are used as games.

SPACE AND IMAGINATION ACTIVITIES

INDIVIDUAL

THE BALL

(If the working space is small, this may have to be carried out by a few members at a time.)

In your own space, climb into a big, opaque imaginary ball. Feel the base under your feet, push your hands out against the front and sides of the ball.

You can see where you want to go, but the ball is heavy, so you'll need to push hard to roll away and round the room. Push, feel your body strain. Once you get going, it will be easier, you'll move along more quickly – but be careful not to roll into anyone else.

Keep moving, hands outstretched, keep pushing until you find a big space near the wall where you can stop moving. Rest, then climb out of the ball and find a chair or a space on the floor and sit and relax.

TOYTOWN

1. Stand in a space and imagine you're a wind-up toy. Think how you would move. Now, hold the key, and hear the sounds as you wind

yourself up. Now, off you go, demonstrating your movement. After a minute or two, the leader says, '*You're winding down now, slower, slower, and stop.*'

2. Repeat – only after a few seconds, react as the leader says '*Oh, there's something wrong – you're going faster – and faster – oh, it's alright, the spring is slowing again – normal speed, slow down – and stop.*'

3. Repeat once more, only this time, the speeding up results in an explosion and the toy is broken. How are you going to show this physically?

MENAGERIE

1. Find a space and imagine you are an animal, but don't say what it is. If you are a bear, are you fierce or cuddly? Are you a showy peacock, a monkey, a shy and gentle deer, or a heavy and ponderous elephant?

   Think yourself into his body and then on the command '*Go*', move about, noticing how you walk and how parts of your body move. Be aware of your paws, your tail, how heavy or strong you are. Be that animal as you move **silently** round the room trying to find others like you, animals with the same movement and body language, then sit, stand or lie beside them making your own little group, but still don't make any noise.

2. Before you repeat the exercise, you may decide to change and become another creature. How differently will you move? This time, think how you would **communicate** as well. Which other animal might be your friend or enemy? Move round as before, only now add some form of communication – it may be a sound or a movement – as you pass other animals.

   When at last you find another of your kind, stand or sit with them and hold a vocal 'conversation' in your animal language.

MOOD WALK

Stand in a space and imagine a mood which you might be in – happy, sad, excited, angry, nervous, bored, cheerful. Walk round by yourself, in any direction, but as you pass someone greet him, still in that mood; then move on, pass three more people before stopping again to talk to them, still exhibiting the mood you chose.

Repeat once more beginning in the same mood, but on the order '*Stop*' each of you should slowly turn a complete circle in your own space. As you do so, you must change your mood completely, before setting off on the exercise again.

Mood Walk Variation

This time, not showing a mood, but a physical change from you as you really are, you're about to move around the room again. Perhaps you're drunk, or carrying a heavy weight, perhaps you've injured a part of your body, or you have poor eyesight, perhaps you're pregnant or have a wooden leg, perhaps you're very old or a child going to a party – just think how you would move.

1. On the word '*Go*' set off, sensing the physical changes you've made to yourself. Do they make you want to be alone in your own space, or do you want to meet people?

2. Repeat your walk, but on the command '*Stop*', say something to the person nearest to you. Can you carry on a conversation with that person?

High and Low

These are status games, which can give some insight into the feelings and body language of characters at different social levels.

1. Everyone is given a playing card. (If cards are not available, members imagine their status as being either 'high' or 'low'). The number on the card rates your status in life, but don't tell anyone else what it is – thus 9 is of a higher status than the ace, which counts as one, and the face cards are even more 'important'. Move round the room, your body and your greeting to anyone you pass showing your status and how you view others around you. On '*stop*' hold a conversation, still in status, with the nearest member.

2. Now change your status – from high to low and vice versa – before you repeat the walk. Note the changes in both your feelings and the physical expression of them. Did you find that 'high status' stands tall, walks smoothly and has controlled speech, while 'low status' curls in on himself as if afraid and moves quickly, almost avoiding contact with others? You may find status relates to a character you play at some time. Which did you prefer? Why?

3. Imagine you are someone else, fact or fiction, either popular or unpopular for whatever reason. Your character can be contemporary or historical, as long as you know something about them.

    Move round the room looking at others in the way you think your character might do, and remembering to move as he/she might. The leader should then call '*stop*', approach one 'character' and hold a conversation with him. The other members try to work out who the leader is talking to. Repeat.

PARTNER/GROUP SPACE ACTIVITIES

These activities will encourage the use of imagination and a spirit of trust and co-operation among the players. On stage, trust and co-operation are most important among actors, as is an awareness of what everyone else around you is doing. During the following games both partners and groups must be aware of the space they occupy, so as to avoid crashing into others, and use their individual spatial awareness to co-ordinate the timing with the other players in their particular game. In the 'Invisible' Games 1 and 2, everyone must 'see' and 'feel' the items they use to play their game. In fact no props may be used in any of the activities in this section. Participants should work so convincingly that anyone watching will 'see' the ball or the rope or whatever it may be, know where it is and be able to link it with the reaction of whoever receives it next.

PARTNERS

INVISIBLE GAMES 1

In a space, imagine that you're playing tennis or badminton, miniature golf, croquet, ping pong, hopscotch, tiddleywinks, marbles, outdoor (ie large enough to walk round) chess, draughts, any game which two can play, but only you and your partner know what the game is.

The leader may stop the action so that some of the partners can 'play' while others guess the game – just how convincing were the actions and was the space awareness right? Repeat.

AIRCRAFT

This game in particular incorporates trust and concentration. Members form partners **A** and **B**. **A** closes his eyes and holds his arms out to simulate an aircraft. **B** must then walk behind him, lightly touching one shoulder, guiding him round the room, speaking quietly only the words '*left*', '*right*' '*forward*', and '*stop*' until they reach their chosen destination across the room.

Then **B** becomes the aircraft and the exercise is repeated.

This can be made more difficult and requires more concentration if the guide stands at the destination to call out his instructions, but in this case, the exercise should only be carried out by a few couples at a time to avoid accidents.

Warm-ups

CROSSING THE BRIDGE

1 Each member **A** takes a partner **B** and stands facing him across the width of the room.

A chair or some form of marker is then placed at either end of the two lines of players, about a metre in front of them. These indicate the beginning and end of very narrow (imaginary) bridges over a deep ravine between each of the couples.

A and **B** then set off at the same time, walking to change places with his partner – but they meet in the middle of their narrow, rickety bridge and each must cross the other to reach his destination without falling into the ravine.

2 Begin this time with each couple (**A** and **B**) on the same side of the 'bridge', which they must cross one at a time because it will not take the weight of two.

A, who is brave, slowly and carefully crosses first. **B** sets off, but once on the bridge, loses courage. **A**, without leaving his place on the far bank, must encourage him to come across safely and successfully. Return across the bridge with **A** and **B** changing character.

Fig 14. "It's OK... just a few more steps..."

IN GROUPS

Divide players into groups of four, five or six.

HOLD IT!

Form Shapes or Tableaux – square, circle, oblong, triangle etc – or a tableau – dance finale, war memorial, copse of trees, wedding photo, christening, monkey family etc, freezing in position when asked to do so, so that others may see their interpretation.

INVISIBLE GAMES 2

Each group must act out one of the following imagining, but not actually having the equipment they need. All can practice first then each group could show their game.

a) **Skipping.** Two hold and turn a rope while the others skip in unison, or enter and leave the skipping line in turn

b) **Team Games.** A ball is passed under or over from whoever headed the team to the last in the line. He then runs to the front to repeat the exercise until the original leader is in place again.

Other team games known to members may be used to provide variety, if they require some invisible item – hoop, bean-bag etc..

c) **Tug of war with another group**.

Were the actions done properly and were they believable?

FORM A MACHINE

Each member of a group imagines himself to be part of a large machine or a cog in one, performing the repetitive movement which that part does. The 'cogs' then come together to work out the machine's continuous pattern of movements into a complete, repeated routine – First, **A**, silently and then **B** while incorporating appropriate vocal sound effects.

Fig 15. Machine!

Warm-ups

RITUALS

Each group works out a rhythmic pattern of movements and sound, which together will make up a ritual. Choose from one of the following:

• Rain Dance	• Welcoming Ceremony	• Haka
• Sacrifice	• Coming of Age Initiation	• Wedding
• Red Indian Pow-wow	• Secret Society Initiation	

In no case should props be used. Knowing that the results will be shown will promote teamwork, confidence and a pooling of ideas among the groups.

Fig 16. Haka!

FURNISHING

This is as more difficult exercise which could take some time! Each group is to furnish a kitchen and they must know where the 'walls' are which form their kitchen area, but they mustn't be physically marked out. Each member chooses one item found in a kitchen – large or small and it may take two to carry it. Then in turn, they carry their item into the space, (remembering its size and weight) setting it in a logical place, until the kitchen is furnished. The task is to remember exactly where the 'walls' are (and the door, of course) to mime how each item is carried in and to remember where everything has been placed. After a practice run, each group performs their 'furnishing' in front of the others, who can judge whether their collective imagination and spatial awareness is effective!

The kitchen can then be dismantled, each item in turn, if members can remember what and where they are. **NB**: It is requires even more concentration if another team has to be the 'furniture removers'.

3 CONCENTRATE!

what this chapter covers...

In this chapter we consider the value of good concentration, and begin to develop techniques to enable performers to do it in the most challenging of situations – on stage and under the glare of an audience...

THE NEED FOR CONCENTRATION

Concentration is an individual skill, one which everyone uses to some degree every day (and especially when acting) but it is a skill which becomes easier with practice. Most of the exercises and activities in this section incorporate some concentration, but the following are specifically designed with this in mind. So, although they may be listed as partner or group work, everyone in fact will be practising the art. Although listed under a specific heading, concentration games could also be used as warm-ups or ice-breakers or before relaxation exercises. Relaxation is generally more effective if it follows tension – and intense concentration does involve a certain amount of both mental and physical tension, even if we may not recognise it at the time. On the other hand, it could be said that people concentrate better if they are relaxed. Whatever your view, there are benefits in either case.

PARTNERS

In the first three exercises the roles should be reversed after a few minutes.

MIRROR IMAGE

This is one of the more well-known exercises. **A** and **B** stand facing each other. **A** then slowly makes movements which **B** must mirror, whether they are physical and/or facial. They may become more complicated, but they must be mirrored accurately. This can be extended into the more difficult:

PUPPETS

A becomes the puppet and **B** the puppeteer, who stands in front of him manipulating the strings which cause him to move.

First they must decide which hand controls the strings for which part of the body – head, arms or feet. The test of concentration lies in being able to co-ordinate the relationship between the hands which hold the strings and the reactive movement. The puppeteer must also be careful to create movements which are physically possible!

Before the change-over, each puppeteer should move his puppet into the space where he's to be stored.

SHADOW DANCING

This encourages partners to be aware of each other and the space they each occupy.

A and **B** stand back to back, with **A** being the 'leader'. Still back to back but without actually touching each other, **A** should create a series of simple movements, which his partner must sense and follow. Any noise in the room will hinder concentration, so making this impossible to do.

CHATTER, CHATTER 1

A and **B**, who sit facing each other, decide on a topic of conversation. At the signal they begin to converse for a minute.

When stopped they turn to sit back to back. **A** is asked 4 questions about his partner which he must answer without looking at him – eg what colour are **B**'s eyes/jacket/shoes/skirt/trousers/hair. Describe his face/tie, is he wearing a watch/jewellery/glasses etc.

Where did the concentration lie – in the conversation or the partner? When the exercise is repeated, the questions should be different.

CHATTER, CHATTER 2

A and **B** sit facing each other. Each thinks of a subject on which he can speak for one minute. At the signal they both talk at the same time without pausing to listen to each other, until the call to stop.

They are then asked if they know what the other was saying and if they found they could listen without losing the thread of what they themselves were saying – something which does require concentration.

ANATOMY

A and **B** stand facing each other. **A** says 'This is my nose', but he touches another part of his body eg his knee. **B** replies by saying, 'This is my knee' while pointing to a *different* part of his body.

Each time the phrase, 'This is my …' refers to the part of the body **last** touched, but the player must touch or point to another part of his anatomy. Many people find this very difficult and it certainly tests one's powers of concentration!

IN GROUPS

PETER RABBIT

This is included for young members of a group, or for adults who have a silly sense of humour and know each other well! A movement is made for each word or phrase. If someone knows the tune, so much the better – thus

Little	*pat the knees once with both hands*
Peter	*hands held out in front, level with the shoulders*
Rabbit	*hands form ears on either side of the head*
Had a flea	*snap fingers once*
Upon his ear	*point to the right ear.*

Repeat these four lines three times – then

So he flicked it and he flicked it	*snap fingers right and left hand*
Until it flew away	*arms to side making flying movements.*

This may be considered too silly to do, but it's not as easy as it looks (especially if it's speeded up the second time). It does need concentration and it always causes laughter!

CHAIN REACTION

Players sit round in a circle placing both hands on a table in front of them, crossing each hand with the player on either side. Thus, your left hand should be in front of the player on your left and their right hand should be in front of you. Your right hand should be in front of the person on your right and their left hand in front of you.

To begin: One person slaps one of his hands on the table and this slap is then repeated by the next hand on his left, and so it continues round the group.

When the circle is completed, repeat the action, beginning with a new person and moving round to the right. Concentration is needed if you are to keep the rhythm going, especially when the movements are speeded up.

MOVING NUMBERS

Members sit in a circle or a line and each says a number in order, beginning at one. They must keep their number throughout the game.

1. The leader then calls out two numbers at random and those players change places – 7 and 12; 3 and 8; 15 and 4 etc.

   Repeat several times.

2. The leader calls out two numbers as before, but after that, the *higher* of the two numbers called must call another number and change places with him each time.

FIZZ – BUZZ

Stage 1. Players sit in a circle and begin counting round in order from 1, but when 5 or any multiple of 5 is reached, the player must say *buzz* instead and then the counting continues round the group.

Stage 2. When players are used to this, count as before, still using *buzz* for 5 and its multiples, but now add the word *fizz* for 7 and any multiple of 7.

So counting will begin 1 2 3 4 *buzz* 6 *fizz* 8 9 *buzz* – and so on.

Anyone failing or hesitating is not using enough concentration – and what happens when you reach 35?

ONE IS KING

This requires great concentration and it involves clapping to an 8 beat rhythm, so it's best to practice that first, step by step.

- To 4 beats, pat the knees twice and clap hands twice and repeat this (8 beats) (ie, *pat, pat, clap, clap, pat, pat, clap, clap*). Repeat these eight beats until all are familiar with the pattern.
- These actions are then repeated as spoken numbers are added over the 1st and 2nd, 5th and 6th beats: eg, if using the numbers one and eight the sequence would be *one, one, –, –, eight, eight, –, –*. That is, every time you pat your knee, a number is spoken.

  The basic sequence in this example would be:

$$\begin{cases} \textit{'one} & \textit{one} & - & - & \textit{eight} & \textit{eight} & - & - \\ \textit{pat} & \textit{pat} & \textit{clap} & \textit{clap} & \textit{pat} & \textit{pat} & \textit{clap} & \textit{clap} \end{cases}\text{'}$$

When this is understood, the players number along the line beginning at one end with the number **One**, and they keep this number as their own. Number **One** is King and he begins the game.

1. He says his number – '*one, one*' as everyone pats out beats 1 and 2 with him, and then everyone claps for beats 3 and 4.

    Then, while all pat out beats 5 and 6 '**One**' calls out another random number – *Ten, Ten* for example, and all clap hands for beats 7 and 8.

2. Whoever is **Ten**, repeats his own number (*Ten, Ten*) as the rhythm line begins again (beats 1 and 2); claps on 3 and 4; then on beats 5 and 6 he calls out *another* number – eg *Seven, Seven* – before all clap the final beats 7 and 8.

3. Number **Seven** then begins the round again by calling out his own number, and so the game continues. Anyone making a mistake must drop out.

It is best to begin slowly, because this game requires much concentration – and don't give up after the first attempt! Try it again over the weeks and everyone will be so accomplished that you can move on to…

ADVANCE THE KING

The game becomes even more challenging if the person who makes a mistake goes to the end of the line, thereby making everyone move up one place and change their number. Whoever is seated in the original number **One** chair when the game ends, is the winner.

4 RELAX...

what this chapter covers...

In the last chapter we looked at the importance of concentration. Closely allied to this is the ability to relax – a relaxed mind concentrates better than a tense one. Since mind and body work together, we will look now at effective ways to relax the body without the need for any complicated or specialised techniques.

THE NEED FOR RELAXATION

The ability to relax is of paramount importance to an actor because body tension affects both movement and voice in a negative way. No actor can work freely and with conviction if his body or mind is tense, for muscles tighten when they should relax and the mind no longer functions efficiently.

Relaxation is an individual, personal skill but it should be practised regularly so that the relaxed state can be called up easily when it is needed – as in the moments just before performance. Relaxation exercises are most effective if practised while lying on the floor, for then the whole body can relax easily, and ten or fifteen minutes should be allowed if the exercise is to be really effective. But unless there's plenty of time, and mats have been brought along with this exercise specifically in mind, the first exercise here may not always be possible during an ordinary group meeting in a hall. With that in mind, other 'loosening up' exercises which can be done while standing or sitting, are also included. However, be careful to pace what you do, especially at first. *Whichever exercise you under-take, never move too quickly and never force your body. If you feel a twinge or an ache, then stop and don't try so hard next time.* Members with a specific medical problem could do the exercise sitting in a chair.

When you relax it is more effective if, instead of just suddenly letting your body flop, you gradually and consciously allow tension to slip away. If you have this muscle control, you can employ it wherever you are without actually having to lie down and you can also target specific muscle areas if necessary. Everyone has his own favourite exercise, but here is a general one to begin with.

Basic relaxation exercise

Find a space. Lie on your back, arms by your side. Stretch out all your body, rather like the points of a star, as if you're trying to reach every point of the room around you. Hold that position for the count of 5 before you allow yourself to return to your former position.

Now close your eyes and start to breathe slowly while you silently talk to your body. See in your mind the top of your head and in thought, tell your scalp and the muscles of your forehead, face and jaw to relax. Take your time. Then slowly relax your neck and shoulders so that you feel as if you're sinking back into a cloud.

Now gradually relax your arms, wrists and hands, pausing each time as you do so, before feeling every other part of your body slowly relax, step by step, until all of you, down to your toes, is relaxed. Continue to breathe gently, letting your mind settle and go quiet – silently repeat a mantra, a word, perhaps, like 'quiet' or 'peace', if it helps.

Rest until you are completely relaxed, physically and mentally. If you do this at home, you could play soft music (and also remember to switch the phone off first!). Lie for a few minutes, concentrating only on your breathing and that warm feeling of peace, before gradually allowing the weight to return to each part of your body in turn, gently stretching your fingers and toes if you feel like it. Rest for a moment, open your eyes and then slowly sit up. Never sit up suddenly – that could make you feel dizzy. Then, when you feel ready, stand up and you're ready for anything!

STANDING EXERCISES

These are designed to free different parts of the body from tension. In each case you should stand comfortably with your feet slightly apart. Repeat each exercise twice:

The whole body

Peepshow

Imagine that you want to see what is happening on the other side of a wall, which is just higher than the top of your head. Put your hands on the top and slowly stretch up on your toes to peer over it. Count 3 as you watch, then somebody turns and you must duck down again. Stand, relax and breathe deeply.

Cleaner

Imagine you are cleaning high windows. You will have to stretch to reach all the corners, but be careful. Now, shake out the cloth and sit in the nearest chair to relax before repeating the exercise, holding the cloth in the other hand.

Colour code

While you are sitting, imagine that you are very cold, think of the colour BLUE. (*pause*).

Now the sun's beginning to shine, things are turning YELLOW, so you can 'unfreeze' a little (*take a breath*).

Now think ORANGE, you're warm now. (*relax a little more*).

Lastly think RED, feel the sun's heat and relax. (*close your eyes and take two deep breaths*).

Remembering the colour code is a quick and easy way of taking your body from tension to a relaxed state – useful as you wait in the wings before going on stage.

Stretch and Melt

Standing, stretch your arms upwards to touch the ceiling. Gradually and smoothly let your arms slowly fall from wrists to shoulders, then down by your sides, as your head drops on to your chest. Allow your spine to melt as your knees relax so that you are standing, drooping forward, your arms hanging loose. Count three, then slowly and carefully straighten your knees and gradually uncurl your spine until your head comes up last and you're standing upright again. Give your body a little shake. Then to loosen your wrists imagine you are shaking water off your hands. To loosen your legs and feet, imagine you have inadvertently walked into a nest of ants – shake them off! Finally, stand tall but with shoulders relaxed and breathe deeply.

HEAD AND NECK AND SHOULDERS

Tension in this part of the body particularly affects speech. To illustrate this, imagine you are standing in a frozen wasteland in just your summer clothes. Now while you are still tensed, say a short poem or a nursery rhyme. Feel how tight your neck and shoulder muscles are – and these are the very muscles which should be relaxed when you speak. What has happened to your voice? It is probably hard and strangled and without much expression. Now stand as if you are warm and happy and completely at ease, and say your verse again. That is how you want to speak, and you do when you're relaxed. An actor must be particularly careful to keep these muscles free at all times and, if necessary, should make sure that they are by loosening them up before going on stage. *Each of the following exercises should be done slowly and only two or three times, with a count of 2 between each movement – and stop if you feel dizzy.*

1. Looking down at the floor, bend your head forward until your chin rests on your chest, return to the normal position, pause, then tilt your head to look at the ceiling, then return to the normal position.
2. Looking ahead, tilt your head to the left ear, straighten up, pause, then tilt towards the right ear, before straightening up again.
3. Turn to look over your left shoulder as far as you can, count three, then return to look forward. Repeat, this time looking over your right shoulder.
4. Shrug your shoulders up and down several times.
5. Stand relaxed, arms by your side. Pull your shoulders as far forward as possible and then pull them back as far as possible, several times.
6. Circle your right arm in a clockwise and then anti clockwise direction. Repeat with the left arm.
7. End by gently shaking loose the upper part of your body, especially your arms and hands – imagine there's sticky paper stuck to your fingers!

POSTURE

To maintain a correct posture, it helps to imagine that there is a thread attached to the top of your head which is holding you erect, but it's not so tight as to make your body tense. Your waist is pulled in, your shoulders square, but never tense. Your head is held steady, with your chin level. Your arms hang loosely by your sides, hands with fingers slightly curled so that your thumb nearly touches your forefinger. Know that your weight and energy are centred. You are standing tall but at ease, so that if you had to move in whichever direction, you could do so easily.

When you stand your feet should be slightly apart, your body weight mainly over one foot, with the other resting on the ground to provide support and balance. You will have to shift your body weight, of course (and this is often done unconsciously) but it should be done so smoothly that no-one would notice. Don't sway or shift your feet frequently, especially when you're on stage, and don't let your legs become tense. However, once you know what your correct posture is, you shouldn't consciously think about it too often.

5 PERFORMANCE SKILLS 1

what this chapter covers…

In this chapter we consider in some detail the first of two essential aspects of performance skill: the *voice*. Games to help with the understanding and control of breathing, articulation and projection are covered here.

VOCAL PERFORMANCE SKILLS

As we have seen you will never perform well on stage if you are tense, and the relaxed state is just as important for voice production as it is for body movement. Your voice will not have the energy needed to project itself or the feelings it must express unless you are relaxed. So, vocal skills begin with a relaxed state, which is important for expression, projection and clarity, and continue with correct breathing from the diaphragm.

BREATH CONTROL

All of us breathe and speak without even thinking about it, but for the actor correct breathing is paramount to successful voice production. Without this skill you'll be unable to speak clearly or express emotions effectively. You'll run out of breath before you reach the end of a speech, or your voice will drop at the end of a sentence. Here are a few basic exercises to help you breathe correctly. Repeat them two or three times. Find a space and stand relaxed and comfortable with your feet slightly apart.

1. Place your hands at the base of your ribs and as you breathe IN feel the muscles draw the ribs upwards, as your diaphragm descends and your stomach muscles relax. As you breathe OUT the stomach muscles contract, the diaphragm rises and the ribs are drawn down and inwards.

Performance Skills 1 (Vocal)

2 Think of all your muscles as being relaxed. As you breathe IN through your nose, lift your heels, then gently drop back on them (but not so suddenly and hard as to jar the spine) and as you do so, say, '*Ha*'. Repeat this several times and your neck area should feel free. If it doesn't, repeat the neck and shoulder exercises on p30, for not only will you get a sore throat if your neck and throat aren't relaxed, but you'll also strain your voice.

3 Timing the breath. Now breathe IN through your nose to a silent count of 3 as you raise your arms to shoulder height.

As you drop your arms again, gently breathe OUT through your mouth, again to the silent count of 3.

Repeat, only this time, hold the inhaled breath (3) before exhaling. As you improve your breath control you can extend the count number, sometimes varying it so that the number when you breathe in is lower than when breathing out eg breathe in to 4, hold 2, breathe out to 6. Repeat, counting the numbers as you exhale, but don't force your breath, control it.

4 Controlling the breath

a This exercise can be done at home when you have a glass of water and a straw to hand. Having inhaled, blow bubbles into the glass at a controlled rate. Next time, control your breath so that the bubbles flow slowly at first before increasing in speed – and vice versa.

b Here is a sentence introduced in stages (shown by /) as more information is added and more breath control required. Say it first a phrase at a time, gradually adding the next phrase until you can complete the whole sentence with expression but without becoming breathless or dropping your voice.

> 'Now let us go walking on this fine spring morning /
> when the sky is blue and the birds are singing /
> flowers bloom bright in the gardens /
> and all is well in the world around us.'

If your breath control is good, you can pause briefly before a new phrase (for expression) but you should not need to catch another breath until you have finished.

5 Snatching a breath is sometimes necessary in speech. Breathe IN and begin to count aloud, snatching a breath through the mouth again after each 6th number. You will feel your chest expand and realise that using better control of your breath in the first place makes speaking long sentences easier that having to snatch a breath like this.

Emotion and breathing

The way you feel will affect the way you breathe, and as an actor you should be aware of this. As you practise this exercise and express the emotion, notice how your muscles react in order to control your breath. Each time take a short breath.

Say the word '**Yes**' – in *excitement*; as if you're *tired; angry; calm*.

Then '**No**' – in *surprise; angrily*; as if you're *disappointed*; as if you're *tired*; as if you're *frightened*.

Whispering also uses the abdominal muscles to control the breath.

Partners

Stand opposite a partner and speaking in short sentences begin a conversation – start with '*I saw what happened*' or '*Why did you leave?*' When you have both spoken once, take a step away from each other. Repeat this, continuing the conversation, still whispering and never raising your voice. You'll find it requires breath control as well as concentration as you try to convey what you're saying across a large space. You'll also find that you must stay relaxed.

The exercise will become more difficult if you stretch your neck forward in an effort to reach your partner verbally, for you'll tighten the muscles in your neck and throat, your voice will sound strained and you may become breathless.

In groups

With 3 or 4 others, act out a short scene from one of the following, with all conversation carried out in whispers:

- Thieves plan and carry out a robbery;
- You have an argument, but you mustn't wake the baby;
- As soldiers, you move in to surprise the (imagined) enemy;
- You have an argument in a church;
- You arrive home very late, but you mustn't wake your parents.

ARTICULATION

Articulation is the ability to speak clearly and fluently, pronouncing words accurately and distinctly and at a pace which allows the listener to hear and understand what you're saying. To do this you use your lips, jaw, tongue, the roof of your mouth and soft palate. The lips and the jaw, in particular, as well as the tongue, should be flexible so that you can speak clearly. The following exercises are useful as a warm-up before speaking lines, but you should begin by freeing all the facial muscles. The exercises given in this section are only a few of the many that there are.

Facial exercises

Facial exercises help mobility both for expression of character and clear speech. These are best done in front of a mirror if one is available – or with a partner if you want some fun! You can do either a) or b), or both.

1. Move your scalp backwards and forwards. Raise your eyebrows, first one and then the other (if you can do it) and then both together. Blink both eyes five times, then wink each eye separately five times. Open your eyes as wide as you can. Wrinkle your nose and using the muscles in your cheeks, try to move it from side to side. Snarl, smile, then yawn.

2. Gently massage your scalp, temples and the sides of your nose, then the back of your neck, the top of your shoulders and your jaw, then yawn. Yawning is a good way of relaxing muscles, especially if you stretch at the same time.

Now move on to the most important parts of the face, which you use when you speak – the lips, jaw and tongue. Say the following without moving either your lips or jaw and you'll see just how important they are – '*Pass Margaret the butter please.*'

Vocal exercises

Repeat one or two of the following exercises several times and notice how each part of your mouth moves to enable you to speak clearly. Repeat the phrases two or three times, but remember that *precision* is important, not how quickly you can say the words.

The Lips. Purse the lips and move them from side to side.

Press your lips together lightly and blow through them so that they vibrate.

Say the sounds *oo, ee, ow* so that your mouth forms a tube, a wide smile and a circle.

Say the following:

- *bay, bee, buy, boh, boo; pat, pep, pip, pop, pup; fay, fee fie, foe fum; way, wee, why, woe, woo*
- *Peggy Babcock, Peggy Babcock*
- *Fiddle piggy, fiddle piggy, fiddle piggy*
- *Boots and shoes lose newness soon*
- *Popping peas and pink pomegranates*
- *Bobby brought some pretty boots for Baby Bertha*

The Jaw. Drop your jaw, then close your mouth quickly so that you make a popping sound.

Drop your jaw, swing it from side to side, then backwards and forwards.

With your mouth closed, chew a large piece of sticky cake.

Say the following:

- *act, art, ash; odd, out, owl, howl, ow! wow!; va, va, van; quack, quack, quack.*
- *Do sharks bark?*
- *Olly the octopus won an Oscar.*
- *Margaret Clark sat in the park.*
- *Your sock will rot if left on the rock.*
- *Harry hangs his hat on the hanger.*

The Tongue. Put out your tongue and touch the end of your nose, then your chin, your left cheek and your right cheek.

Pretend you're clearing sticky crumbs from behind all your teeth in turn.

Purse your lips and curl your tongue out through them.

With your jaw dropped, flap your tongue quickly behind your teeth.

Say the following, noticing what your tongue is doing:

- *day, dee, dye, doh, do; no, no no; they, thee, thy, then; ray, ree, rye, row roo.*
- *Grey clay held the clue*
- *David dared little Larry twist the twine tighter*
- *Rose limped along the track*
- *I tied my kite to a little tree*

The Soft Palate is the back of the roof of your mouth. It lowers when you make certain sounds, such as *m, n* or *ng*. Say *ah* and slowly change to saying *ng*. Can you feel what's happening? Try saying *long, strong, ring, dancing, performing, humming*.

All together now... Any tongue twister will help you maintain mobility of your mouth and will encourage clear articulation, provided that you remember to say each word clearly rather than trying to say them all quickly. Here are a few to say three times, and you'll know many more:

- *Mrs Smith's fish sauce shop*
- *pack a copper kettle*
- *imagine managing an imaginary menagerie*
- *double bubble gum bubbles double*
- *the slim spider slid slowly sideways*
- *for sheep soup, shoot sheep*
- *freshly fried fresh flesh*
- *three grey geese in a green field grazing*
- *eleven benevolent elephants*
- *red lolly, yellow lorry* (yes, the second word is different from the last!)

Good articulation is especially important to the actor who may have to speak in a dialect, which means you will have to work harder to get that dialect correct. A member of an audience who can not understand what you are saying or who misses dialogue, for whatever reason, soon loses interest.

But an actor does not only need to speak clearly to communicate effectively, he must also speak with feeling and expression.

With this in mind, it is a good idea to read aloud whenever you can – play readings are the perfect opportunity, or perhaps read the bedtime story to a child – you won't get better practice than that. You could also read aloud some of the lyrics from the works of Gilbert and Sullivan – or better still, sing them. Your clarity and articulation will certainly improve if you do.

But remember that when you speak as an actor the expression in your voice will come from an understanding of the character you are playing, and the thoughts and emotion behind the words you are saying.

VOCAL EXPRESSION

When a playwright writes his dialogue, he knows what he wants his characters to communicate, and he hopes that the actors will be able to interpret this through the way in which they deliver the lines. There are six ways of doing this – through pitch, inflection, power, pace, the tone of the voice and through an intelligent use of pauses. If you're in tune with your character in the play you'll probably express yourself well automatically, just as you do every day when you speak. But if you know something about the mechanics behind vocal expression, you'll not only speak with clarity but also with conviction.

PITCH

In ordinary conversation the voice is generally pitched at a medium level, but it may, for some reason (and sometimes subconsciously) change to high or low. As an actor with a script, you must know when this would occur and why, so that by varying pitch you can express yourself more clearly. High and Low pitch can suggest:

- **An emotion**. A high pitch generally indicates a high emotion, excitement, hysteria, incandescent anger; a low pitch could indicate sorrow, tiredness, boredom, secrecy, misery and even menace.

    Using first high and then low pitch, say '*What have you done?*' '*Come over here.*' Can you hear and sense the difference in feeling?

- **A different meaning**. A change of pitch on a single word can change the emphasis in a sentence, changing not only the sense of a character's emotion or intention but also the meaning itself.

    Say each of the following sentences, each time emphasising a different word in turn and you'll notice five totally different meanings:

    'We're going to the theatre on Monday night.'
    'We're going to the theatre on Monday night.
    'We're going to the theatre on Monday night.
    'We're going to the theatre on Monday night.
    'We're going to the theatre on Monday night.

- **Information in parenthesis** – an extra piece of information which could be left out of the sentence without losing the original intention (here giving information about Posey) – for example:

    'Posey, [*who's working in the green house*], is Clay's elder daughter.'

    The pitch of the voice for the phrase in italics should be slightly lower.

INFLECTION

This is not unlike pitch, for it is a varying of pitch on one word to indicate the sense of what you're saying, the variation being on an upward or downward note.

The final word in a statement generally has a downward inflection – *'I'm going home now.'* Make sure that, as an actor, you don't allow your voice to rise at the end of a statement, because that suggests that the sentence is unfinished, or even that it is a question.

POWER

This, too, is closely allied to pitch. It doesn't necessarily mean that your voice grows louder, but more that it grows in strength. This can happen as a climax at the end of a speech, or it can grow gradually during the speech as strength of feeling grows. You will feel this if you read aloud part of a speech from Shakespeare's 'Julius Caesar' when Brutus speaks of him:

> 'As Caesar loved me, I weep for him; as he was fortunate, I rejoice at it; as he was valiant, I honour him; but as he was ambitious, I slew him.'

PACE

When you study a script you will generally find that the pace and rhythm of the lines will be dictated by the writer. He will have worked and reworked them until he has achieved the emotional effect he wants. That is why you should learn scripted words as they are written and not paraphrase them.

Varying the pace, especially in a long speech, will keep the dialogue fresh, interesting and meaningful, but you'll only find the pace at which you should deliver the lines through study of the text.

TONE

The tone of your voice will indicate your mood or emotion, and it will colour the words you're saying. For example, the tone in which you ask the question, *'Will you do it for me?'* will indicate whether you're being demanding or forceful, kind or cajoling, as it will with a simple command like, *'Come here.'*

In everyday life you instinctively vary the pitch, tone and pace of what you say, as you will if you read the simple examples on the next page with a partner.

Scenario 1	Scenario 2
A. Bill Scott's over there.	**B**. Stand still.
B. Bill Scott?	**A**. What?
A. Bill Scott.	**B**. Don't move.
B. Not the Bill Scott.	**A**. Why?
A. Bill Scott, the actor.	**B**. There's a snake.
B. Bill Scott, the actor from 'Dancers'?	**A**. No! Where?
A. 'Skaters.'	**B**. There, by your foot.
B. I'm sure it was 'Dancers'.	**A**. Oh, no!
A. No, 'Skaters.'	**B**. Now, move back slowly.
B. Are you sure?	**A**. I daren't.
A. Yes. He was the one who got married.	**B**. You must – slowly.
B. No, he didn't.	**A**. I'll … one step.
A. Yes, don't you remember?	**B**. Now another.
B. That wasn't Bill Scott.	**A**. Er …I've done it.
A. It was. We'll ask him, OK?	**B**. Now, let's look.
B. Yes, we will. Where is he?	**A**. I daren't.
A. He's over …Oh, he's gone!	**B**. Now … Ah, sorry. It's a stick.

As an actor studying a script, you must understand the character's attitude, thoughts, feelings and intention behind the words before you can hope to say them correctly and convincingly. If you do this you'll say the lines as the playwright meant them to be said without even having to consider which techniques you're using to get it right.

Pauses

A slight pause can be used rather like vocal punctuation, to help you phrase sentences so that they make sense. (They also remind you to breathe!) In text they are marked as commas (a brief pause) and full stops (slightly longer) and they act as a guide, but you may also need to pause where there is no printed punctuation.

You may need to pause fractionally (/) for a dramatic effect. This may be to give the audience a second to think about what you're going to say – 'The quality of mercy / is not strained,' or have said – 'She is a murderer / you know.'

You may also use a pause to indicate emotion – confusion or anger, tiredness or dejection, for example: 'I'm so tired / I can hardly think.' 'I don't know / what /to do.'

Some playwrights, like Harold Pinter, use the pause to great effect. They are printed as such in the script. They contain a wealth of meaning and unspoken thought, and the actor(s) concerned must convey this in the silence. It is a special skill and as an actor you really have to identify with the character's feelings, and time (feel) the pause exactly, so that you end it before it becomes embarrassing.

Unscripted pause. There is one other occasion when you should pause, but it will never be scripted and will generally only happen during a comedy. This is when you hold your line rather than speak it, because the audience is laughing at a previous line or piece of action. You must always pause long enough for the audience to enjoy their laughter, don't speak through it. If you do, your lines won't be heard, the point of your saying them will be missed and the audience will feel cheated because they weren't allowed time to enjoy a funny moment. With practice, you'll 'feel' when you should pick up the dialogue again. Just be aware that next time the laugh might not come in the same place. Every audience is different

PROJECTION

Projection is the very necessary art of reaching every member of the audience vocally, and it is one thing which every new actor worries about. One thing you must not do is strain physically to 'throw' your voice to the back of the room. Good projection comes, above all, from **preparation, concentration, intention and confidence**.

PREPARATION

You prepare yourself **mentally**, over a period of time, by studying the lines and knowing what you are going to say. Through rehearsal, you'll also know how you're going to say them, because, hopefully, you will have become your character. You must concentrate on this during rehearsal and again once you're on stage.

Before the show, you prepare yourself **physically** by breathing deeply, relaxing your neck, throat and upper body and by warming up your voice in the dressing room – sing up and down the scales perhaps. It helps if you can lubricate your throat by drinking some water before you go on stage – water, not milk. As any trained singer will tell you, milk has the effect of increasing any mucus in the throat, so restricting the work of the larynx and vocal chords. In the wings, you consciously relax yourself and prepare to switch on your energy the minute you go on stage. Once there, make sure that you breathe from the diaphragm and keep concentrating.

INTENTION

Your intention is to share your character and his part in the play with your audience, and you intend to do this well. When you speak you are not just going to try to reach the audience, you are going to *include* them – even the little old lady sitting in the back row. After all, they have taken the trouble to come and support you. You must keep in mind that you intend your voice to reach whichever part of the hall you decide on, and know that you will succeed without having to shout.

CONFIDENCE

These preparations will bring with them the confidence you need to project your voice. Remind yourself that because of all that preparation you have done, everyone will hear what you say because *you know what you are doing, and what you are going to say is worth hearing*. So take a deep breath and believe in yourself. Switch on the energy in your voice on the very first word. That says 'I have confidence in myself,' and if the audience believes that, they'll relax and listen. No-one in that hall wants you to fail, and many of them know that they would never have the courage to do what you're about to do – act on a stage. Stop worrying, go for it and your own confidence will carry your voice to the back of the hall with ease.

This advice also applies to any public speaking. As long as you are organised, well prepared and know your subject well, the confidence that knowledge brings will enable you to speak clearly and with conviction, whatever the subject.

6 PERFORMANCE SKILLS 2

what this chapter covers...

The second half of our discussion of performance skills deals with physical performance, and in this chapter we will consider how to create characters through posture, movement and gesture and how body language can drastically affect the meaning of the words in the script.

PHYSICAL PERFORMANCE SKILLS

There are many aspects to performing, and although, having read the script, you may know what the play is about, the script itself is not the whole story. The playwright has created the plot, the characters and the dialogue, but it is the actor, with his director, who brings it all to life. So how do you do that?

BODY LANGUAGE

Speech is the most obvious means of communication, but although we may not realise it, body language is equally important. Body language means movements made by the body, generally involuntary, which give obvious or subliminal signals, clues to our intention/motivation, and our reaction to any emotion, person or situation. Millions of years ago, before language as we know it came into being, man's thoughts and feelings were expressed through noises, movement and gesture. Early research carried out in the 1950s by Albert Mehrabian, a researcher in body language, showed that in most cases today communication is still, on average, 45% verbal and 55% non-verbal. So it is not only how you say things, but also what your body is indicating when you say them, for body language is closely linked to thought and feeling. That's why telephone calls and emails are not as satisfactory as speaking to someone face to face, for you're not able to gauge their non-verbal reaction to what you're saying.

Our bodies react to a pattern of '**thought → emotion → action**' and that action is a conscious or unconscious movement of some kind. For example, when you feel nervous, you may bite your lip; when you're happy, you smile; your brow furrows when you're worried or angry. You give these signals without even thinking about it. Here's a quick experiment which may prove the point (answers are at the foot of the page):

1. Think of a picture you've seen, remember the detail. Now, while you were thinking, where did you look?
2. Now think of a tune that you know, hear it in your head. Where did you look this time?
3. Try to recall an emotion, a time when you had very strong, personal feelings about something. Think about it. Where did you look?
4. Finally, when you're told to begin, talk to yourself, just start a little monologue, until you're told to stop. It doesn't matter what you say, because everybody else will be talking too.

So parts of your body, in this case your eyes, move even when you're not aware of it.

EYE CONTACT

While on the subject of eye movement, do remember that eye contact is an important and vital way of reading another person's intention, attitude and even to some extent, their thoughts. As an actor you should, where possible, maintain eye contact when you speak directly to someone on stage. There is nothing worse than talking to someone who looks at your forehead or over the top of your head when he addresses you. Try this group exercise which will illustrate the importance of eye contact in relation to emotion as well as communication.

TESTING EYE CONTACT

Everyone stands in a space and then:

1. Walk round the room, but as you do so, don't look at anyone, avoid their gaze and make a mental note of how you feel.

Answers to experiment above

1. *The chances are that you looked up to your left.*
2. *You probably looked either to your right or left with your head slightly tilted*
3. *Most people look down to their right.*
4. *Did you look down left towards the floor? Many people do.*

Performance Skills 2 (Physical)

[2] Now walk round again, but this time look at everyone you pass. How do you feel this time – probably happier and part of the group again. It's unlikely that you'll feel as isolated and alone as you did when you avoided eye contact.

FACIAL EXPRESSION

Facial expressions are also a guide to thought and emotion and we often consciously change these to hide what we're actually feeling – as when talking to small children in a worrying situation.

It goes without saying, therefore, that when you're in a play, your body language will go a long way toward helping you bring your new character to life, but you must know what the character's thoughts and emotions are, so that your body has the motivation it needs to respond in the correct way.

CREATING CHARACTER PHYSICALLY

Try now to create a new 'you' physically.

POSTURE

When you are acting, your own natural posture may need to change. Stand in a space as yourself and then decide on your new 'you'. Will you stand tall and upright, or craven and hollow-chested? What is your status in life, for status is also something which could affect your body language. Where is your centre of energy? Do you 'lead' with your chin so that you look down on everyone, or do you stick out your stomach and swagger? Remember the animals? (p16). What kind of animal might characterise you? Are you a serious, wise owl, still but watchful for most of the time, or a heavy hippo? Are you light on your feet or do you walk with a heavy tread, for even the way you walk gives an indication of character as well as age, mood and motivation. But do try to be accurate in your movements – you only have to ask a six-year old to walk like an old person to see how misinformed some interpretations can be!

WALKING

The following exercises show how thought and intention/motivation affect your posture and the way you move. Find a space and when told to, move across the room in character after pausing to consider what your thoughts are when you're told that:

1. You are shy but you have to enter a room full of strangers at a party.
2. On the way home from shopping it begins to rain heavily, but you have no umbrella.
3. You are old and you must pass a group of rowdy teenagers on the pavement.
4. You arrive home having just won a medal at the Olympics.
5. On a holiday beach you're the only one who isn't sun-tanned.
6. You have had too much to drink, but you don't want anyone to know.

The way you moved probably changed when you heard the instruction, which in turn altered your thoughts and intention.

Conversely your body language can affect how you feel:

Stand at ease in a space, and as yourself, imagine that your source of energy is in your chest. Now that you are conscious of it, let that energy give you the power to walk round the room, wherever you want to. You will be walking tall as you normally do.

1. Now, mince around as if you are very prim and proper. Has this affected the way the rest of your body moves and what you're feeling or thinking?
2. Walk now with a loping action. Did you find that your thoughts changed as well as your posture?
3. Move with the weight on your heels as you take each step. How did you feel? Did your character change? What sort of person did you imagine you might be?

Gesture

As the new character you are creating, are you the sort of person who stands, arms folded in a defensive position, or an expansive man who sticks his thumbs in his braces? Do you show nervousness by shifting from one foot to the other? We use gesture in many ways, sometimes

- To express emotion (holding hands up to the face in shock or raising a fist in anger).
- In conventional ways (shaking hands in greeting or waving goodbye).
- As an expression of an inner emotion which we may even be trying to hide (wringing hands in anxiety, twitching or drumming fingers impatiently). These can be useful to an actor when used in character,

as long as they're not over-used or too repetitive. No audience likes to watch an actor who doesn't seem able to speak without using his hands.

But even gestures themselves can alter your body movement as your intention strengthens or changes. To illustrate:

Imagine your friend is standing a short distance away and beckon him to come to you in the following ways (in each case he will not respond) a) hesitantly; b) as an ordinary demand; c) be a little more determined; d) angrily.

Did your body change – tense perhaps – as your intention to make him obey increased?

ENTRANCES AND EXITS

To sustain characterisation, you should know your motivation and how you're feeling before you make an entrance or leave the stage. Don't enter and then suddenly remember why you're there. Try moving correctly as you say the following phrases. If you work as a group of four, you could each take a different adverb while using the same phrase and the others can tell you if you're convincing.

Enter an imaginary room saying:

- *'I'm here.'*   a) happily; b) reluctantly; c) fearfully; d) in exasperation.

- *'Where is he?'*   a) excitedly; b) angrily; c) anxiously; d) tearfully.

- *'I've something to say.'*   a) as a matter of fact; b) angrily; c) happily; d) as a confession;

Exits. In a group as before, each speaker begins by sitting, pausing for a second and then leaving after saying:

- *'I'll go.'*   a) in exasperation; b) lazily; c) in anticipation; d) angrily.

- *'I'll phone tomorrow.'*   a) happily; b) sleepily; c) angrily; d) tearfully.

- *'Goodnight.'*   a) sleepily; b) tearfully; c) angrily; d) lovingly.

SITTING

Remember that not only the nature of your character, but also the period in which the play is set will dictate how you sit. Men and women each sit in a different way – men generally with knees apart, women feet together or legs crossed. Victorian ladies did not sit with legs crossed. New actors sometimes even find the very act of sitting difficult. Unless you actually move across to the seat immediately before you sit, you may find yourself shuffling backwards or sideways if you're not aware of just how near you are to the edge of the chair. So, if you know you have to sit, during rehearsal you should note where the chair is and align yourself near to it, and when standing in front of it just feel the edge of the seat behind your legs. Note, too, on the dress rehearsal, just how high or low it is. If it's a very low chair, you may have to sit on the edge or very upright if you're not to feel inferior to another whose seat is higher. Whether you lower yourself gently into a chair, or flop will depend on your character!

ENERGY

This is something every actor needs and should display from his very first entrance. It is an almost indefinable quality, and it doesn't mean that you burst on to the stage like a madman or say your lines with great power. Rather, your energy lights you from within, making the audience want to watch you. It will show in your voice as a certainty, which comes from really knowing your character and your lines. Just as someone will smile if you smile at him, so if you show through this 'energy' that you are in control, the audience will believe in you, sit back and know they're in safe hands. They feel what you feel, so don't show your nervousness or embarrassment on stage! Notice the times at the beginning of a rehearsal when a lack of energy is quite obvious. Actors droop on the stage and say the lines as if they're bored or tired, even though they're not. But if you pretend that was just a warm-up and begin again, this time remembering to 'switch on' your life, the scene will take on life as well and it will be interesting to watch.

Most of the activities in the following chapters on Improvisation and Mime will help you practise many different ways of expressing character through body language. But before you proceed to this, we should perhaps consider the links between memory and imagination.

MEMORY AND IMAGINATION

Memory and imagination are often so inextricably linked in the mind that it can be difficult for an actor to analyse which of these helped in his recreation of a scene or a character. But occasionally it is interesting to analyse which of these two attributes are the stronger in one's makeup. Both can be made stronger with practice. The following exercise can involve either or both, depending on the individual.

Mind walk

Members sit and follow instructions, painting pictures in their minds without physically moving. The instructions should be given quietly and slowly, allowing members time to create in their minds the journey they're making.

> 'You're going on an imaginary journey in your mind, just a walk, but you'll remember the details of it, so close your eyes and relax.
>
> Before you set off, look round and see where you are, feel the ground beneath your feet, know how you're feeling
>
> (*pause*)
>
> Now, you're walking along a public highway, notice what it's like, see what's on either side of you, notice the air, the atmosphere, the people if there are any. As you walk on, notice the sky, what it's like.
>
> (*pause*)
>
> The area around you is changing a little now, the road narrows, but you don't mind that, you keep walking. You can see some buildings in the distance. You walk towards them and you find that there's one in particular which interests you more than the others. You walk towards it and then you just stand at look at it.
>
> (*pause*)
>
> Look at the detail there – the walls, the windows, the colours, the surroundings, all the other things you can see. You see a door. Look at it. What's it like? Notice the detail.
>
> Then you see that it's partly open. Oh, you must just go and look inside before you go back home. So you walk up to the door and

give it a slight push. It opens wider, so you peep inside and you see … Now hold that vision, remember it.

(*pause*)

Now, I want you to take a deep breath, then slowly open your eyes.

(*pause*)

Now, tell us about your walk.'

The results, when the 'walks' are recounted, always prove to be varied and interesting and in some the detail is very precise. Analysis by each member can give an insight into whether what he 'saw' was pure imagination, accurate recall of a factual event, or a mixture of both. There can be a wide variation among members, but it may serve to remind players that when they act, they can use both of these skills to advantage.

7 CREATIVE DRAMA

what this chapter covers...

With group members now relaxed, concentrating and aware of the fundamentals of acting, it is time to get creative! In this chapter we will look at the value of spontaneity and mime in creating engaging drama from very simple ideas.

IMPROVISATION AND MIME

A leader suggesting any form of improvisation or mime may be met by groans and shudders from members who shrink into themselves and exclaim, 'Oh, no. I can't do that!' And maybe even the leader, if he has never tried it for himself, won't realise just how valuable an activity it can be, for it enriches the drama experience and can be most enjoyable. It frees the mind, and confidence grows along with imagination.

If you think about it, many people improvise in a small way every day, without ever realising that's what they are doing. Have you never made up a convincing reason (excuse) when you've been late for an appointment or done something which you shouldn't have done; or improvised a movement by suddenly bending to tie a shoelace (even though you may be wearing slip-ons) when you don't want someone to notice you? Young children improvise all the time. Listen to them play in a Wendy House or round a dressing up box, or watch them use a cardboard box in so many different ways.

IMPROVISATION

Improvisation in its simplest form is acting spontaneously, using memory recall and your imagination, everyday language and physical movement – and making it up as you go along. That's all it is. But in a drama group situation it's great fun and a valuable activity. It brings to those who practise it more understanding of life and of themselves, and through this, a confidence which allows the nervous to try something new, the reticent to become more outgoing and it even, perhaps, makes the intolerant more tolerant. It also has the advantage of being new and original, unique even, every time it's undertaken. Improvisation

- Allows participants to explore characters other than their own and situations they may never have been in, or ever will be.

- Increases the ability to understand emotions, both your own and those of others, and provides an opportunity to express them, as well as thoughts and ideas, in an articulate way. If an actor becomes practised in doing this using his own words, he'll bring this ability into any study of a script written by someone else.

- Encourages spontaneity, so improving language skills and the ability to respond quickly in an appropriate and coherent manner.

- Encourages interaction with others, improving the ability to share and co-operate and exchange ideas – something everyone needs, especially on the stage.

- Develops the imagination, which is a particularly useful skill in acting, and encourages creativity.

- Used in conjunction with a play which is in rehearsal, it may enable both the producer and the player to come to a deeper understanding of a character, a scene or even of the dialogue itself.

When using Improvisation, you as the leader should

- Always make sure that the work attempted is introduced and carried out in a friendly, cooperative, caring way. The group is, after all, a socially based group, and nobody should be made to do what they don't want to do. If you could start the ball rolling by taking part yourself, your enthusiasm should encourage all members to join in the fun.

- Know what you hope members will achieve from any activity and how you may be able to help them carry it forward.

- Start with simple ideas, varying the type of exercise as time progresses, and be prepared to carry over any which promises to grow into an 'event' – such as a duologue or group work which needs more time to perfect. It might even become a sketch or short play – although this may not have been the aim of the exercise.

- Be sure to give instructions clearly and precisely before the activity begins, making sure that members understand exactly what they're to do before you give them the signal to begin.

- Know the approximate time you want to give to that particular exercise.

- Move round, noting work which is good and which may serve as an example, helping where members may appear to be in difficulty.

- Be prepared to stop the exercise if it's foundering.

- Warn when it's nearly time to end, before finally giving a clear instruction to stop.

- Allow time for members to show what they've done, bearing in mind that there may not be enough time for everyone to do so. At first, the 'showing' should take place in the area where it was practised, but as members become more aware of positioning in relation to their audience, a 'stage space' could be adopted at one end of the room where all partner or group improvisation is shown.

It will make your work much easier if you transfer some of the activities, especially those with multiple ideas, into card format, as has sometimes been illustrated here. It takes time, but once done they are ready for use whenever needed and this format will save time in future explanation and organisation. It also means that members could use them in the event of the organiser being absent or busy elsewhere. Naturally you will also add many of your own ideas to those given, as well as instigating other original activities.

MIME

This art form is the perfect example of the specific use of body language to convey ideas and thought. Through it you can tell stories, express thoughts, feelings and intention so well that anyone watching knows exactly what is happening and no words are necessary. Some of the exercises already used employ mime to some degree, but in this chapter we look specifically at mime and see how its skills link to the actor's craft. The first activities are mime in its simplest form.

Individual mime

Everyone joins in and stands near a chair. Following your instructions, they will mime the following:

Tea-time

You're standing in the kitchen and you're going to make a cup of tea and then, when it's ready, sit down and drink it. Begin. Watch, and when they've finished ask if anyone forgot any detail, such as switching on the kettle in the first place!

Post!

Everyone sits. They're waiting for a postal delivery. On your signal, they go to the door to pick up/receive the post before returning to the chair to open it. They must show by their reaction what this item of post contained and the effect it has on them.

1. A letter has just dropped through your letterbox. Go and get it!
2. Here's the postman. He's brought you a very heavy parcel.

If it's a parcel, did they remember to open and close the door when collecting it? Did the 'parcel' appear to be heavy?

Supermarket

(If the group is large, work no more than ten at a time. A small table should be placed at one end of the room to represent the check-out – it could have a member of staff there or be a self service check-out.) Imagine you're doing the weekly shopping. Take your trolley or basket and move round, taking no more than eight goods from the shelves, moving in such a way as to show what they are. You ask for help if necessary – but remember that this is mime and you may not speak! Sit down at the end to show you're home. Discuss how effective the mimes were.

'Shore' thing

Everyone sits along the longest side of the room, facing across to a part of the 'beach' which will be their own space. Then you give the instruction:

> At last you have five minutes to go down to the beach and you're determined to enjoy yourself. How will you spend that short time, paddling, playing in the sand, beach-combing, gazing out to sea? You decide. Now go and have fun!

After a few minutes call members back to their seats and discuss what they did.

REWIND

Having completed any of the last mimes, players might then rewind them, as you rewind a video-tape. It would be best to begin this exercise by repeating the chosen mime first – probably the simplest one. Trying to remember a sequence of moves backwards needs a great deal of concentration and should be done slowly. This forms a useful introduction to some of the group mimes later.

COLLECTIVE MIME

MIME CIRCLE

(This can be done while the group is sitting).

Mime circle involves physical expressions of feelings and movement, which arise out of true memory, imagination or, more often, imagination coloured by some true or mistaken information.

The group, sitting in a circle, is told that they are going to mime passing an object from one to the other round the circle. They must indicate what the object is through movement and expression, and others must judge how accurate their mimes are. You, as leader will tell them what the object is, but this will change as it is slowly passed from hand to hand. The change-over should be done slowly and deliberately so that both the action and reaction are clearly seen when one thing changes to another.

For example, the object could start off as '*a heavy parcel ... now it's a baby rabbit ... it's changed to a sticky sweet*'. It is best if the leader has already listed the objects he'll mention so that there's no break in the flow. The list is limited only by the leader's imagination, but here are a few ideas to get you started:

wet pondweed	a worm	hedgehog	baby rabbit
full cup of tea	heavy box	pin	kitten
diamond ring	ticking bomb	a butterfly	a squishy cake
perfumed flower	a bowl of soup	a beetle	a bouquet
perfumed sachet	bird in a cage	smelly socks	a snake

THE WALK

Members move round the room, listening to your voice and reacting appropriately. This is best used after a warm up when members move to stand in a space, or if sitting, they are told to put on (imaginary) light sandals, for they're going for a walk. Remember to watch the participants, describe what you 'see' vividly and time the instructions so that they have time to see/feel what you describe and have time to do what you say.

> 'Now, off you go. It's a lovely sunny day and you're strolling along a country lane – see those pretty flowers, hear the birds – there's a field gate, open it and walk along that path beside the corn – it's rather narrow but you'll manage. Oh no, the ground's rather wet here – and there's a large puddle.

(pause while they negotiate it)

Now the path is very stony, can you feel the sharp stones? – but carry on – look to your right, there's an orchard, don't the apples look good? You're hungry now – there's nobody around; why don't you pick one – have you room for another in your pocket? Take a few, but then perhaps you'd better move on, someone might come.

(pause)

Oh no, the only way out is through the hedge – look, there's a small hole – can you get through? – oh, it's hard

(pause)

but yes, you'll just make it – your sandal, it's got caught – rescue it.

(pause)

Oh no! There's someone coming – hurry! Get out of this field – come on, hurry! – you've come to a stream – you'll have to cross it, but there's no bridge.

(pause)

Look – stepping stones, you'll have to use those – careful *(pause)*

Fig 17. Picking and storing apples.

Go on, you'll just make it – one final jump – there! You're on firm ground again. It's beginning to rain now – which way is home? stand and make sure – yes, it's that way – hurry, there's a storm brewing – quickly – hurry – have you got the apples? – keep going – there's your garden – up the path – through the door – phew, you're home at last! Find a chair, sit and take off those wet sandals! (*pause*) What an adventure!

There are many variations of this – through mud and over gates, exploring a ruin or trying to hitch a lift, tiptoeing through rows of plants or over a ploughed field, crossing a rickety bridge or ending up in quicksand! It is suggested that you only use the last idea when members are physically fit, know each other well and the hall floor is clean! The only limitations will be in the leader's mind, but plan the route and pitfalls first, know where you're going and don't put your members in any situation where they may really get hurt!

PARTNER AND GROUP MIMES

The following mimes are short but form a good introduction to the longer activities suggested later.

ACTION!

The group is divided into two equal lines **A** and **B**, standing about two metres away from each other. Using only gesture and facial expression, a member from each line in turn (**A** then **B**) should mime doing something in detail and their partner, having guessed what it is, must repeat every movement. Ideas include:

> cutting a lemon in half and eating it; enjoying a bar of chocolate;
> chopping an onion; seeing a wasp buzzing nearby; removing a sock;
> angrily telling the partner to leave; beckoning him to come;
> mixing and frying a pancake; making chips; opening champagne;
> polishing an item of silver; cleaning shoes; crocheting;
> stitching embroidery; plaiting an imaginary child's hair;
> arranging flowers in a vase; resetting a stopped clock.

The more complicated the mime, the better, but all the detail must be observed for it to be repeated correctly.

(The obvious extensions to this are the 'What's my Line?' game or Charades.)

Rhymes and Stories

The following lend themselves to mime. The topics are given out to the relevant number of members needed, who work and then 'show' to the others who must guess the rhyme or story. The number of participants is shown in brackets. (It is easier for the organiser if the topics are on cards, a sample of which is shown below.)

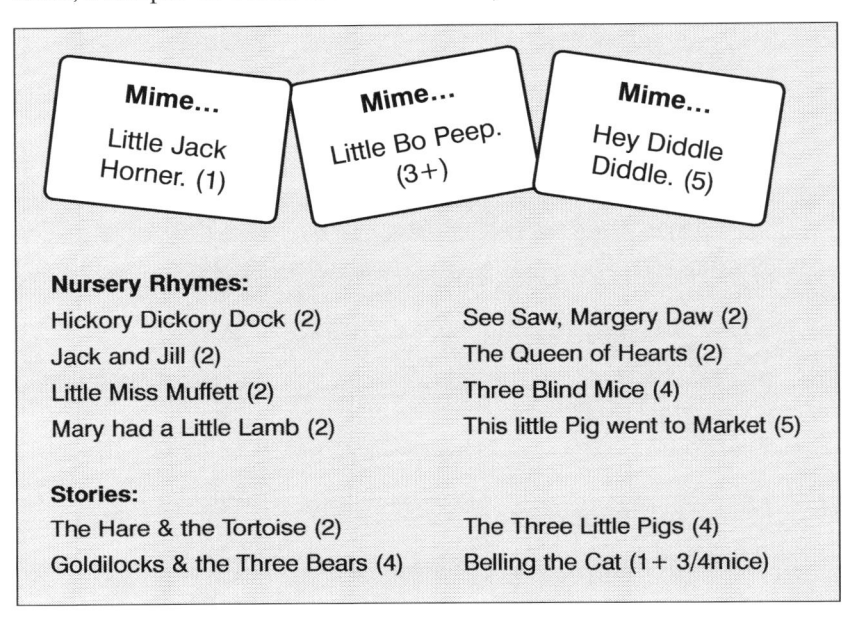

Mime... Little Jack Horner. (1)

Mime... Little Bo Peep. (3+)

Mime... Hey Diddle Diddle. (5)

Nursery Rhymes:

Hickory Dickory Dock (2)	See Saw, Margery Daw (2)
Jack and Jill (2)	The Queen of Hearts (2)
Little Miss Muffett (2)	Three Blind Mice (4)
Mary had a Little Lamb (2)	This little Pig went to Market (5)

Stories:

The Hare & the Tortoise (2)	The Three Little Pigs (4)
Goldilocks & the Three Bears (4)	Belling the Cat (1 + 3/4mice)

Mini-scenes for groups of 3-6

Each of the following should be mimed, although a short discussion is allowed first for the participants to draft out the story, which should be kept short and to the point. The actions should be detailed and clear, showing through mime only, action and reaction. It is best if little choice of title is given from the following:

- The picnic
- Arctic adventure
- School sports day
- Rescue!
- Lost in the desert
- Accident!
- Cream teas
- Escape from gaol
- Soldiers on parade
- Clara's wedding

Commentary

Only one in the group may speak, the others mime the action which will be commentated on (where no 'end' is obvious, one should be devised):

Creative Drama

• The Fashion Parade	• Egg & spoon Race	• Boat Race
• Jane visits the Doctor	• The Boys hang a Picture	• Pitching Tent
• Defusing a Bomb	• A Visit to the Hairdresser	• Disco Time
• Victorian Laundry Day		

SILENT MOVIES

These activities are great fun and they encourage all the acting skills, especially concentration. It is an opportunity for players to over-act, to use melodramatic movement and extravagant gesture to portray emotion. Ideally, the group should be of no more than 3 or 4 and each character should be clearly defined. The instruction should be to 'keep it simple', for both timing and co-ordination between the actors is essential.

Allow five minutes for 'casting' and storyline discussion before mime rehearsal begins. The movie itself should take no more than 4 or 5 minutes. Use only one title or give a choice of two or three. After rehearsal, the groups show their movie.

1 Begin by acting out the story as a straight-forward silent movie. Only when this has been seen should you build in 2 and then 3 (below) — then players will understand why everything had to be simple! For example, the dumb waiter might do no more than give each customer the wrong plate and then have to return to change the order — not so easily done backwards! Choose from one of the following:

• The Dumb Waiter	• A Bar in the Wild West
• The Pipe of Peace.	• The Intruder
• Tramp in Love	• The Stripper
• The Tea Dance.	• Stop Thief!
• Shoot-out	• The Proposal

2 Now repeat the movie, with the first half of the action being in slow motion, the second half at speed.

3 Play the movie and then rewind it — best if the exercise 'rewind' (p55) has been used during a previous session.

8 IMPROVISED DRAMA

what this chapter covers…

In this final chapter, we draw together all the skills learned in this section of the book. Here participants are given starting points for a huge variety of drama improvisations which will test what they have learned and help them to develop even further.

IMPROVISED DRAMA

This section is a logical progression from mime and many, in fact, find the activities easier to do because they can speak! Now that dialogue comes into play, the scope for drama widens considerably. Players have more freedom to experiment and the resulting scenes have an added depth of thought and emotion, as well as more interplay of relationships – not only in the scene but between the participants themselves. The examples given have all been found to work and if presented as cards (such as those illustrated), can be used over a period of time.

INDIVIDUAL ACTIVITIES

The following ideas encourage spontaneity and confidence because everyone works at once, and each knows that he's less likely to be noticed or his voice heard. The result may be noisy, but as leader, you can monitor what's happening and occasionally stop the group, to watch or listen to someone who is willing to show his work.

CONVERSATIONS

Everyone finds a space and imagines that they have a mobile phone in their pockets. On the signal, each 'answers' his phone and carries on a conversation. We only hear one side, of course, but his words and attitude should be so convincing that the listener can guess what the conversation's about – which is what members do when they're asked to stop to watch someone continue his phone call.

SOAP BOX

Everyone has their own favourite topic about which they have very firm views, whether anyone else agrees or not.

1 At a signal everyone addresses the room as if he were on his soapbox, while at the same time listening for the Leader's instruction to stop. Then in turn, one or two can continue, speaking to members of the group who will actually be listening to him!

2 This time the 'speakers' should use a controlling emotion as they 'lecture'. It may be love, hate, envy, anger, fear – whatever they choose – and the topic can be serious or frivolous. Again, choose those who wish to share their thoughts. (You may allow 'heckling' if you judge that the speaker can handle it, but that may be better left until the group has consolidated and the players are more confident.)

FOCUS

Each member stands in a space facing his chair, but a short distance away from it. He must then imagine that it is whatever he is told it is, but he has to pass it, deal with it or use it. He must show that he believes it's real, by using appropriate body language and speech. The leader then suggests to the group one of the following. It may be:

• a snake on a rock	• an abandoned baby in a pram
• a fierce dog	• a shopping bag left on a path
• a bird in a cage	• a deaf man asleep in a wheelchair
• a large heavy sealed box	• a tiger before the open door of its cage
• a throne.	• an abandoned car with its engine running

PARTNERS

Improvisation is most satisfactory if it's created with a partner or as a member of a group, for it gives the opportunity for shared involvement and interaction. The ideas in the first 'vocal' section result in a conversation, often confrontational, but without a great deal of action, (which is what, at this stage, they are designed to do) and it's wisest only to use one or two at a time, perhaps after a physical warm up. In each case the participants are **A** and **B** who should take it in turns to lead the scene. Partnerships should change frequently.

With a partner – Vocal

Questions, questions!

A and **B** hold a conversation using only a) questions or b) just one or two words until one fails to reply correctly. They are timed and the winning partnership is that which can converse longest without a mistake.

Pardon?

A and **B** hold a conversation, but speak only in gibberish (unintelligible speech) or sounds. This gives players practice in expressing themselves using only inflection, tone of voice and pace.

One line Duologue

An exercise in spontaneity where a single line starts a conversation. There should be no previous discussion and the organiser decides whether it is **A** or **B** who says the line. Here are some ideas to start with:

'Look at the mud on your shoes!'	'What are you doing here?'
'I've got a message for you.'	'I'm sorry about last night.'
'What a waste of money.'	'Why didn't you tell me?'
'Where have you been?'	'Call yourself a friend'
'I wasn't expecting you.'	'I've changed my mind.'
'What's the matter?'	'I'm going out.'
'You look awful!'	'Hey look over there.'
'Must you do that now?'	'You read my diary?'
'Don't be such a misery.'	'Stop picking on me.'
'I'm fed up with you.'	'Why is it always my fault?'

Character duologue

This time each participant takes on a character, preferably one who has some relationship with the other. When they have decided on their characters, the duologue begins with two lines:

A. I'm just going out.	**B**. Do you have to?
A. Come over here.	**B** No.
A. That looks nice.	**B**. I've just bought it.
A. Look at that!	**B** It's mine.
A What are you doing?	**B** Mind your own business.
A I've lost my job.	**B** What did you do?

A I'm telling my mum.
A Leave me alone!
A Don't, it's dangerous!
A. I don't want to go.

B I don't care
B. But you've got to listen.
B. Who says?
B. But you must!

SITUATION DUOLOGUE

In every case **A** and **B** must bear in mind what he really believes, wants (his intention), or has to do, and he may need to change the approach in his argument in order to try to achieve this. There should be no discussion before the duologue begins and it doesn't matter who speaks first.

A short scene takes place in a:

Shop	**A** intends to buy an item of clothing. **B** tries to persuade him/her otherwise.
Hospital	**A** visits a sleepy, long lost friend. **B** doesn't remember who it is.
Surgery	**A** anxiously visits the doctor. **B**, as the doctor, diagnoses and advises.
Hairdresser's	**A** wants the usual haircut. **B** wants him/her to try the latest style.
Waiting Room	**A** wants to join the armed forces. **B** is against the idea.
Street	**A** wants to see a murder film. **B** prefers a comedy at another cinema.
Office	**A** is trying to finish some work. **B** wants to gossip.
Aeroplane	**A**, about to do a parachute jump, refuses. **B** has to persuade him to do it.
Tent	**A** awakes and hearing a noise wants to leave. **B** refuses.
Gym	**A** is using some equipment. **B** insists he/she is using it incorrectly.
Shared bedroom	**A** is always untidy. **B** likes everything neat.
Bank	There's a robbery. **A** wants to fight back. **B** wants to run.

CHARACTER DRIVEN DUOLOGUES

These activities focus on the movement and body language of character and the motivation behind it, as well as the necessary language skills. Members work in twos as before, **A** and **B**, and they are told their characters. Then the location of a scene is given – each couple could have the same location or choice of another might be given. Either **A** or **B** may start the conversation, but they must stay in character.

	CONFRONTATION	
Scene	**A**	**B**
A party	is pompous and conceited	is nervous and shy
A Pub	just wants a quiet drink	is drunk
School Reunion	has just left school	is a very old ex-pupil
On board ship	is going on holiday	is an escaped prisoner
Hospital ward	is a frightened patient	is a pessimistic visitor
Library	is stiff and serious librarian	is very deaf
Expensive Wine Bar	is rich but dirty	is a well-mannered waiter
Disco	loves the loud music	hates everything about it
Art Gallery	is intent on stealing a picture	is security Guard
Bedroom	just out of the bath finds	who is a burglar

MOODS

In this exercise body language sets the mood, for what happens between **A** and **B** is suggested by the way they stand or sit and there is no rule as to who starts the conversation. Each member takes a card (unseen) from the pack (illustrated opposite) and, without conferring, takes the position which is suggested there. The physical attitude they take should suggest to each a mood or an intention, and each should decide in his own mind – without conferring – what that may be, and he should know why he feels like that. Both the reply to the first line

Improvised Drama

> **Mood...** Sits back, eyes closed.
>
> **Mood...** Sits, (mime) reading.
>
> **Mood...** Sits, staring into space.

Sits forward, hands dropped down between his knees.
Sits, drumming fingers on the arm of the chair/his knee.
Sit facing partner, arms folded.
Sits watching partner.
Stands with his back to partner, looking into the distance.
Sits, knees together, hand clasped in lap.
Leans back in chair, legs extended.
Stands, eyes closed, hands over his mouth.
Stands, arms tightly folded.
Stand behind partner, touching left shoulder.
Stand, a finger in each ear.
Stand, pointing to the distance.
Stands, hands in pockets, watching partner.
Stand, fists bunched.
Stand, wringing hands together.
Stands, hands on hips.
Stand clapping hands held high.
Bends, pointing to the floor.
Pacing up and down.
Walking slowly, hands behind back.
Kneels, head bowed.

and to what follows should be logical. The action must begin with a pause, which is broken by either **A** or **B**.

'I SAID ...'

This activity adds further variety to this type of work, and extends the imagination. Either **A** or **B** assumes the position on a card from the 'Moods' pack (above) while his partner starts the duologue by using a random line given to him by the organiser from the list given from One line Duologue on p62.

LEAVING

Players **A** and **B** should assume a character with some relationship to the other – parent & child; brother & sister; husband & wife; employer & employee; teacher & pupil; pop star & manager; dance teacher & pupil; nurse & matron. Action begins with one announcing '*I'm leaving.*'

GROUP WORK

It is best to start with simple ideas and small groups, (which are changed for each topic) especially when working with members who may not have done improvisation before. At first, participants may prefer to act as themselves, for in that way they find it easier to concentrate on 'the story' they have been given to work on. In time, they may wish to assume another character even though they may not have been directed to do so. Begin with open titles and remind the players that, as far as possible, they should keep their 'plays' short (no more than five minutes) and try to give the action an introduction (beginning), an event (a middle) and a resolution (an end).

Each section begins with examples of instruction for the players, but as they become more experienced this shouldn't be necessary. Pooling of ideas from within each group is much more valuable. Topics may be taken from a variety of sources. Scenes may be based on

'OPEN' IDEAS

GIBBERISH

(Group of 3). **A** and **B** are working when they have an accident or something goes wrong. **C** arrives and they must convey to him what has happened and what they want him to do, but they may only speak 'gibberish'. It helps if **A** and **B** have used this 'language' from the beginning and established made-up words for certain objects, although **C** will not know these.

STOP, THIEF!

(Group of 3). **A** leaves a supermarket. **B** follows him and accuses him of theft. He is taken before **C**, the Manager. What happens? It should not have been decided whether he is guilty or not, so that players gain practice in using argument and persuasion to resolve the situation.

THE VISITOR

(Group of 4 – 3 family members and 1 visitor who is brought home by a member of the family.) The character of the visitor is very important. What effect does his arrival have on everyone?

THE OUTSIDER

(A cohesive group of 4, +1) Consider what makes an outsider. Is he a stranger, a joker, a tramp, over-eager to please or embarrassing (like 'The Office's David Brent)? Is the group jealous of him, is he a prude or is he just 'strange' in some other way? Is he eventually accepted and if so, why/how?

FURTHER 'OPEN' IDEAS

The following topics may require more planning but give excellent opportunities for collaboration and imagination. Encourage players to invest in original thought and not just to create the obvious (see 'The Journey', below). With some characterisation, the activity generally results in 'a good story'. Be prepared to allow a little more time for these:

THE JOURNEY

This can be factual or magical. Decide on the reason and historical period of travel, the mode of transport, the destination and the outcome. You may, for example, decide to journey into another time, or into space where you discover an inhabited planet. In this case, starting as if you're sitting in a time/space capsule about to land is one way of setting the scene. This formation also makes a satisfying way to end this type of play – if you decide (and are able) to return home, of course!

OTHER STARTING POINTS

The following could be used as stimuli for activities similar to 'The Journey', above.

- The Picnic
- A Stormy Night
- The Phone Call
- Treasure!
- The Swindle
- My Slave
- Pirate
- Shipwreck
- The Strike
- 'Must Buy' – Plan and film a TV advert for a new product.

LOCATIONS

THE LIFT

As an imaginary character you enter a lift with others and act out what happens when the lift stops between floors and twenty minutes elapses (not in real time!) before it begins to move again. Do your reactions reveal/match your character? How do you behave when you finally reach the safety of a floor?

THE QUEUE

As some character other than yourself, you stand in a line as if waiting in a very slow supermarket queue. How do you behave and interact with others? What do you say?

THE PLATFORM

Before acting out this scene, assume a character and a mood which you may be in. You're standing on a station platform on the way to an important meeting and the train's very late. How do you feel? What, if anything, do you do and say? How does the scene end?

FURTHER IDEAS

In each of the following, the premise is that one or two players will enter the location and disturb or change the ambience of the others already there:

• A Restaurant	• A Waiting Room	• A Launderette
• A Pub	• A Police Station	• A Haunted Building
• A Beach	• A Railway Carriage	• An Old People's Home
• A Park Bench	• An Infants' Classroom	• A Race Meeting

PLAY-MAKING

This particular kind of simple improvisation, which involves action and reaction, can be repeated many times. To facilitate this, the leader would be wise to create a set of cards – see opposite – which suggest characters and scenarios.

Note: With members new to improvisation, it may be best to use these cards in three stages:

     1   Players have only character card, A, and the scenario D.

Improvised Drama

2 Next time they add a 'mood' card. (ABD).

3 Each player has a character, intention and mood to bring to the given scene (ABCD)

continued on p70

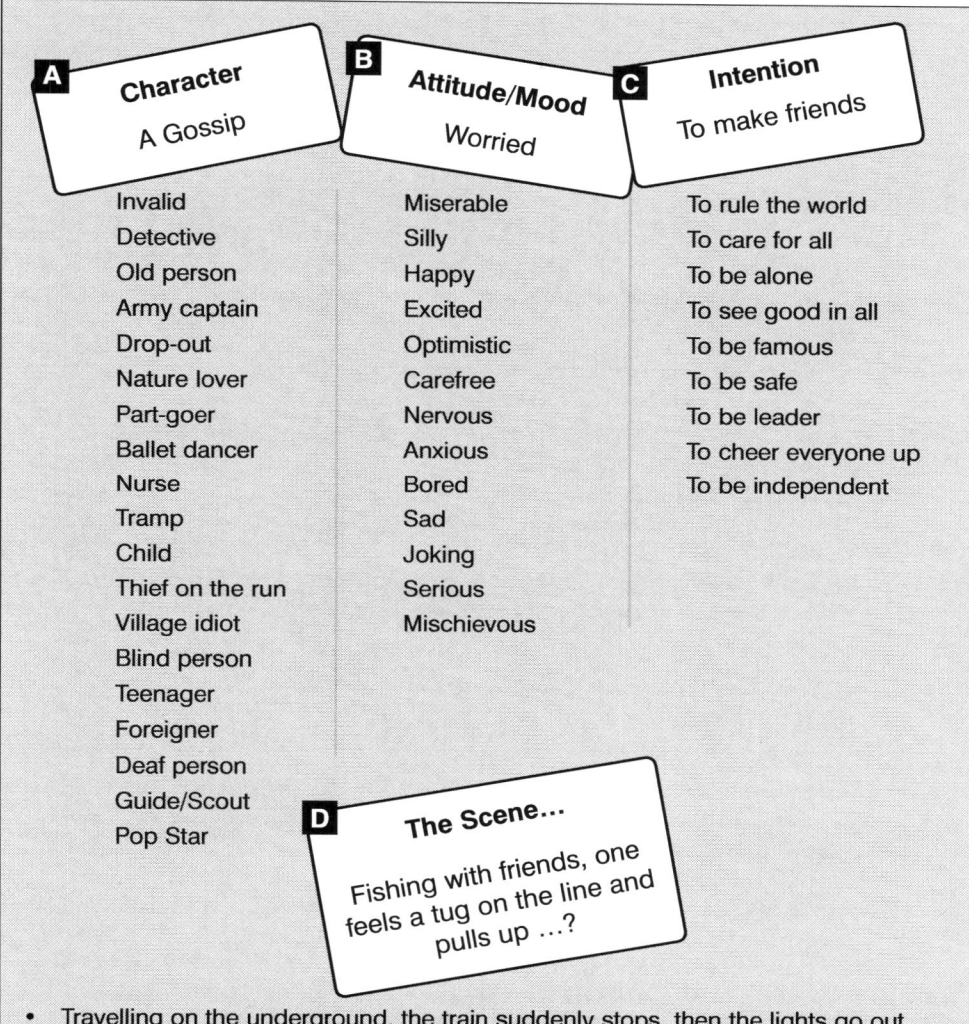

A Character
A Gossip

B Attitude/Mood
Worried

C Intention
To make friends

Character	Attitude/Mood	Intention
Invalid	Miserable	To rule the world
Detective	Silly	To care for all
Old person	Happy	To be alone
Army captain	Excited	To see good in all
Drop-out	Optimistic	To be famous
Nature lover	Carefree	To be safe
Part-goer	Nervous	To be leader
Ballet dancer	Anxious	To cheer everyone up
Nurse	Bored	To be independent
Tramp	Sad	
Child	Joking	
Thief on the run	Serious	
Village idiot	Mischievous	
Blind person		
Teenager		
Foreigner		
Deaf person		
Guide/Scout		
Pop Star		

D The Scene...
Fishing with friends, one feels a tug on the line and pulls up ...?

- Travelling on the underground, the train suddenly stops, then the lights go out ...
- Visiting a busy fair, there's suddenly a shout from a stall nearby ...
- Walking along a quiet country lane, you look over a field gate and see ...?
- Exploring beach caves after a picnic, you discover that you can't find the entrance ...
- Visiting a waxworks, from the corner of your eye, you see one figure move ...
- In the office, someone says 'What's wrong with X?' (a colleague).
- You're looking down on a coffin at an historical dig, when the lid begins to move ...
- You're in your garden with friends when a stranger appears. He looks worried ...
- In a restaurant with friends, you see a man at a nearby table behaving suspiciously ...

When each group of 3, 4 or 5 has been formed, players take an individual card from the relevant pile placed face down. Then each group is given a previously unseen scenario card. This sets the scene which the characters must play out. The groups should choose titles for their 'plays', which should last no more than 5 minutes. Allow 10 minutes preparation time before each group shows their 'play' to the others, their 'audience'. This has proved to be a popular activity, which provides fun and instruction as well as encouraging co-operation and use of the imagination.

As a matter of interest, when using all three cards there are 28,000 combinations in this game. If you used 10 a week, 52 weeks a year, it would take you over 53 years to work through them all!

A Theme

After discussion the groups enact a short scene which illustrate the chosen theme from the Seven Deadly Sins and other like subjects:

• Avarice	• Gluttony	• Lust	• Sloth
• Pride	• Envy	• Anger	• Ambition
• Revenge	• Fear	• Power	• Hope
• Fidelity	• Conflict	• Sacrifice	

For example: Sacrifice. This can be thought of a moral dilemma. Perhaps one character is 'sacrificed' for the good of the majority. The setting may be historic, domestic, recreational, in war or a working environment.

Using known material as a starting point

Fables

The idea when using a story or fable is *not* to recreate the story as it is, but to modernise it or use it to illustrate the meaning behind it. Here are just a few suggestions to use as examples:

The Boy Who Cried Wolf so many times that no-one believed him when he told the truth.

The Ugly Duckling, once an outcast, but who proved to be a beautiful swan.

The Lion and the Mouse who showed that even the most humble could help the powerful.

The Hare and the Tortoise – slow and steady achieves a result.

QUOTATIONS

These may come from many sources including verse, fiction or plays. The task in the following is to create a scene suggested by the lines by commenting, asking a question or changing the original thought. Note that you are *not* trying to continue the writer's original idea, but simply using his lines as a springboard for your own interpretation. It does not matter whether you know where the quotes come from, or what comes next. In fact, *not* knowing – and having to take the lines just on face value – may well lead to much more creative improvisations!

- *'Tyger, Tyger, burning bright*
  In the forest of the night …' (William Blake)
  What shall we do about it?

- *'The Owl and the Pussycat*
  Went to sea in a beautiful pea-green boat…' (Edward Lear)
  But they landed on the wrong island!

- *'Please Sir, can I have some more?'* said Oliver. (Dickens, 'Oliver Twist').
  What shall we do with this child?

- *'Do you remember an inn, Miranda,*
  Do you remember an inn?' ('Tarantella', Hilaire Belloc)
  Now, what happened there?

- *'When shall we three meet again?'* (The Three Witches in Shakespeare's 'Macbeth') The challenge here is to take the spell from the original verse (Act iv sc I) and use it (update it if you wish), but set the scene in another time and place. It could be in the present, it could be anywhere in the world, but the players should know what they hope to achieve by casting the spell. – and do they succeed?

So many of Shakespeare's lines have become part of our language and they make a good starting point for improvisation. We owe the following to him although there are many more, of course. The task is, as before, to create a scene, but this time make the quoted lines the *last* ones in your play:

- *'Neither a borrower nor a lender be,*
  For loan oft loses both itself and friend.' (Polonius to his son in 'Hamlet', Act 1, sc III.)

- *'The course of true love never did run smooth ...'* (Lysander, 'Midsummer Night's Dream' Act 1, sc I.)

- *'O beware, my lord, of jealousy*
  It is the green-eyed monster ...' (Iago warns Othello against his wife, Act 3, sc III.)

- *'Good night, good night, parting is such sweet sorrow ...'* (Juliet, 'Romeo and Juliet' Act 2, sc II.)

TEXTS FOR LARGE GROUPS

These are more ambitious projects for experienced players, but they generally prove to be absorbing topics for the whole group to work on. The work will spread over more than one session, and may even, if later scripted, grow into a public performance! These improvisations call for more thought, planning and discussion as well as characterisation and collaboration.

SNOW WHITE AND THE SEVEN DWARFS

This story could be improvised as it was written, unless the group wants a challenge. In that case, the hero, heroine and the dwarfs could be 'modernised' in some way, as could the work they do, and someone other than a witch could represent the evil in the story – but good should overcome evil in the end.

THE PIED PIPER OF HAMELIN

(by Robert Browning). This could also become a play in its own right. It could begin with groups of townspeople complaining, with another group forming the Council, the Pied Piper as the principal player and others playing the rats and the children.

VISITING

'Welcome,' said their hospitable host ... stepping forward to announce them, 'welcome, gentlemen, to Manor Farm.' (Dickens, 'Pickwick Papers).

This last line in Chapter 5 of Dickens' novel relates to the arrival of Pickwick and his friends at the home of Mr Wardle after a rather adventurous carriage journey, but you are free to interpret the welcome as you wish. Manor Farm may be anywhere and your host can be anyone. Why are you visiting? Act out a scene exploring why you are at the farm and what happens during your visit.

JABBERWOCKY

(from 'Alice through the Looking Glass' by Lewis Carroll). This may be an unexpected suggestion but it can prove to bring out a great deal of imagination as players become 'slithy toves' and 'mome raths'. It is an opportunity to enter the world of fantasy and there is no right or wrong in any interpretation. A Narrator reads the verse as players enact it, so that it becomes a mimed presentation. The use of music greatly adds to the finished scenes.

CRIME AND PUNISHMENT

No, not Dostoevsky! In the following, we take children's stories and set them in a court scene. You will need to appoint a Judge, defence and prosecuting barristers as well as the complainant, the accused, the jury and its foreman. You may even call witnesses. Again, much planning will be needed, but the characterisation should be fun!

Goldilocks and the Three Bears. Father Bear takes Goldilocks to court for breaking and entering.

The Three Little Pigs accuse the Wolf of harassment and take him to court.

Members should be encouraged to think up their own scenarios too — any well-known story or characters can be used as a basis for the creation of mini-plays. The more familiar the original text is, the more fun the group can have with showing the characters in sticky situations that the original author never intended! (However, be aware that if you wish to work any of these ideas up for public performance that some modern characters are very heavily protected as trademarks.)

COSTUME/PROPERTIES WHICH SUGGEST A CHARACTER

The use of one item of clothing or a prop is a useful way of concentrating on characterisation within an improvised scene. In preparation, the leader should supply a variety of objects, or each member could be asked to bring an item — it must be possible to wear the extra clothing over the members' own clothes. Using a book of raffle tickets, each item is numbered with its 'twin' number being folded and placed ready for the draw. Having formed the separate groups, each player draws a ticket and then must use the item he 'wins' to create his character. You may wish to use both an item of clothing and a prop if the groups are small. The scene must be woven round the characters who form the group. Some items you may wish to use are listed over:

> Scarf, shawl, skirts of various lengths, raincoat, jacket, apron, dressing gown, waistcoat – the brighter the better, ankle socks, Wellingtons, slippers, hiking boots, boater, bowler hat, child's cap, baseball cap, clown's hat, ladies hats, bonnets, tiara, pith helmet, cowboy hat.
>
> Handbag, shopping trolley, walking stick, briefcase, basket, magnifying glass, sunglasses, goggles, sweeping brush, bucket, shovel, mop, umbrella, notebook & pencil, sack, dog lead, a cane, fairy wand, – anything which may stir the imagination!

THE BOSS

These are activities to encourage leadership skills and are best used when members are accustomed to working together. There will be among the membership those who always take a leading role or who organise the others. Here, it's suggested that once individual groups have been formed, the leader chooses someone other than the usual 'organiser' from each group who must then be 'in charge'. They will be given instructions, which they must carry out. Knowing the players, the leader can best judge who might be given this opportunity to take an organising position.

- As Captain of a sports team, you must teach your group a routine, which will engender positive thinking before the game.
- You are organising a Fashion Show. Rehearse your new models ready to walk along the cat-walk in (imaginary) garments ready for the display.
- You are leader of a group practising movements which will bring to them calmness and control.
- You have to teach a short dance routine to your group for a musical.
- You are Officer in Charge of some new Army recruits and you must teach them some basic drill.
- Your group is on a secret mission, one which will surprise the enemy. Show them how to advance without being seen and practice this as a team.
- You must teach your group 'The Dance of the Robots'.
- You are in charge of a Keep Fit team about to give a Fitness display. Practice the routine together.
- You are in charge of a Roman galley ship. You must train your oarsmen to move in time by teaching them a rhythmic chant to say as they row.
- As a Circus Trainer, you must teach your group some simple circus skills.

CONCLUSION

All the suggestions for Improvisation above are just that – suggestions. Some will work better than others and many will give rise to other ideas within the group, so that before long you will have a list of ideas of your own which over time, you'll be able to repeat, with variations. Some may even grow into performance material, which is why, if you can, you should keep a record of the work you do. The use of appropriate music, although not suggested here, does help performance. Indeed, some music may even inspire a topic for exciting improvisation, whether it is a modern song or classical music such as that in the compilation for Disney's 'Fantasia'. It is certainly worth using music for a change.

It is to be expected that at first you will make mistakes in your presentation. You'll find it difficult to keep unscripted conversation going without talking over each other; your positioning will lack foresight and you may even work with your back to the audience; you'll mask each other; you may find it hard to work to a satisfactory ending in the given time. But don't despair. These are all part of the learning curve and should prove valuable. Both you and your fellow members who'll be your audience, will recognise these errors, although no criticism will be given – and if it is, it should be no more than a suggestion – 'next time why not try / it might be better if…' Everyone learns best through practical experience, and this along with mutual observation will, over a period of time, teach you some of the stagecraft skills you'll need in performance. As you become more practised, you will remember that the needs of the audience must be taken into account too, particularly in relation to the actual staging and positioning of the actors they're watching.

Above all, however, remember that 'the play's the thing', so the story, with character relationship and interaction, is most important, especially in later group work. Whenever you work together, whether it's to rehearse a show or to 'improvise' you'll have fun and that is the whole point of starting an amateur drama group in the first place.

APPENDIX: USEFUL WEBSITES

Hypertext links to these and other sites can be found on the Eyelevel Books website at www.eyelevelbooks.co.uk/drama

LEGAL AND STATUTORY BODIES

Information on **lotteries and gaming**
www.bbc.co.uk/actionnetwork   or   www.gbgb.org.uk

Health & Safety Executive, gives practical advice on such matters.
www.hse.gov.uk

Arts Council England is the national development agency for the arts in England and Wales, distributing public money from Government and the National Lottery
www.artscouncil.org.uk
The Scottish Arts Council can be found at   www.scottisharts.org.uk
The Arts Council of Northern Ireland is at   www.artscouncil-ni.org

The Charity Commission is the regulator for charities in England and Wales, for information on charitable status   www.charity-commission.gov.uk
The Office of the Scottish Charity Regulator can be found at www.oscr.org.uk
At the time of writing, there is no equivalent body in Northern Ireland

The **MCPS-PRS Alliance** is the home of the world's best songwriters, composers and music publishers and has information on licences for public performances of copyright music. See also www.ppluk.com (the Phonographic Performance Limited site)   www.mcps-prs-alliance.co.uk/

SOURCES OF GENERAL HELP AND INSPIRATION

The British and International Federation of Festivals for Music, Speech and Dance.   www.festivals.demon.co.uk

Online Sound Effects has a library of useful FX at   www.sounddogs.com

UK theatre web is worth checking out if you own your own venue www.uktw.co.uk

The Independent Theatre Council (ITC) is the UK's leading management association for the performing arts, representing around 700 organisations across the UK.   www.itc-arts.org.

Amdram is a free website for the amateur theatre community. It includes free resources for groups and individuals interested in amateur theatre. www.amdram.co.uk

National Operatic and Dramatic Association gives a shared voice to the amateur theatre sector, helps amateur societies and individuals achieve the highest standards of best practice and performance and provides leadership and advice to enable the amateur theatre sector to tackle the challenges and opportunities of the 21st century. www.noda.org.uk

NAYT (National Association of Youth Theatres) supports the development of youth theatre activity through training, advocacy, participation programmes and information services. www.nayt.org.uk

Sources of Plays and Other Material

Nick Hern Books is the UK's leading specialist publisher of plays, screenplays and theatrebooks
www.nickhernbooks.co.uk

Samuel French Ltd is THE theatre bookshop and supplier of scripts
www.samuelfrench-london.co.uk

Josef Weinberger is another major supplier of play scripts, musicals and opera
www.josef-weinberger.com

The Internet Theatre Bookshop has a catalogue of plays and texts and a whole lot more! www.stageplays.co.uk

Index

A
Articulation 35

B
Body language 43
Breath control 32

C
Choosing 'teams' 4, 10
concentration 4, 9, 10, 12, 13, 18, 19, 21, 22, 23, 24, 25, 26, 27, 34, 41, 55, 59
Confidence 42

D
Dress rehearsal 48

E
Emotion 34
Energy 48
Entrances and Exits 47
Eye contact 44

F
Facial exercises 35
Facial expression 45

G
Gesture 46
Group work 66

H
Head and neck and shoulders 30

I
ice-breakers 4, 12, 13, 15, 22
imagination 4, 5, 9, 15, 18, 21, 49, 50, 51, 52, 55, 65, 67, 70, 73, 74, 79
Improvisation 51
Improvised drama 60
Intention 42

M
Membership 10, 11, 74
Memory and Imagination 49
Mime 51, 53

P
partnered activity 11
Pauses 40
Physical performance skills 43
Posture 30, 45
Preparation 41
Producer 52
Projection 41

R
relaxation 27
relaxation exercise 28

S
Sitting 48
Skills 9
Space Activities 4, 14, 18
Standing exercises 28

T
Texts for large groups 72
Tips for the leader 4, 10

U
useful websites 77

V
Vocal exercises 35
Vocal expression 38
Vocal performance skills 32

W
Walking 45
Warm-ups 4, 12, 13, 15, 17, 19, 21, 22

Printed in Great Britain
by Amazon